the focus on the family®
WOMEN'S MINISTRY
guide

Gospel Light

PUBLISHED BY GOSPEL LIGHT
VENTURA, CALIFORNIA, U.S.A.
PRINTED IN THE U.S.A.

Gospel Light is a Christian publisher dedicated to serving the local church. We believe God's vision for Gospel Light is to provide church leaders with biblical, user-friendly materials that will help them evangelize, disciple and minister to children, youth and families.

It is our prayer that this Gospel Light resource will help you discover biblical truth for your own life and help you minister to others. May God richly bless you.

For a free catalog of resources from Gospel Light, please call your Christian supplier or contact us at 1-800-4-GOSPEL *or* www.gospellight.com.

PUBLISHING STAFF
William T. Greig, Publisher • **Dr. Elmer L. Towns,** Senior Consulting Publisher • **Natalie Clark,** Product Line Manager • **Pam Weston,** Managing Editor • **Alex Field,** Associate Editor • **Jessie Minassian,** Assistant Editor • **Bayard Taylor, M.Div.,** Senior Editor, Biblical and Theological Issues • **Rosanne Moreland,** Cover and Internal Designer • **Debbie Alsdorf,** Contributing Writer

ISBN 0-8307-3338-8
© 2004 Focus on the Family
All rights reserved.
Printed in the U.S.A.

Any omission of credits is unintentional. The publisher requests documentation for future printings.

Unless otherwise indicated, all Scripture quotations are taken from the *Holy Bible, New International Version*®. Copyright © 1973, 1978, 1984 by International Bible Society. Used by permission of Zondervan Publishing House. All rights reserved.

Other version used

KJV—King James Version. Authorized King James Version.

contents

contents

The Purpose of the Focus on the Family Women's Series

And this is my prayer: that your love may abound more and more in knowledge and depth of insight, so that you may be able to discern what is best and may be pure and blameless until the day of Christ, filled with the fruit of righteousness that comes through Jesus Christ—to the glory and praise of God.

Philippians 1:9-11

The goal of this series is to help women identify who they are, based on their unique nature and in the light of God's Word. We hope that each woman who is touched by this series will understand her heavenly Father's unfathomable love for her and that her life has a divine purpose and value. This series also has a secondary goal: That as women pursue their relationship with God, they will also understand the importance of building relationships with other women to enrich their own lives and grow personally, as well as to help others understand their God-given worth and purpose.

The Focus on the Family Women's Ministry Guide

Women today have an innate need to connect, build relationships and express themselves. Providing women with opportunities to meet together and experience knowing each other through purposeful relationships, events and activities will allow them to build and deepen bonds of friendship, soften their hearts toward God and encourage growth in all areas of life.

Time is precious and women spend it carefully. Investing the hours and effort to make an event, study or activity memorable and significant will reap many benefits for all involved. When planning activities for the women you serve, have a clear purpose in mind beyond filling a space in the calendar. Prayerfully consider how each activity will enable you to reach out and draw women in to a place where they feel welcome, accepted and special in God's sight. Understand the needs and interests of those you want to reach with a particular experience. Choose leaders, speakers and hostesses who can clearly communicate the purpose of the event, study or activity and who can represent Christ with integrity as they prepare for and serve the women. With these individuals in place, make the effort to create nothing but the best for them. This means praying for them, planning well and planning ahead.

PREPARING FOR *Ministry*

chapter one

DEVELOPING YOUR OWN
Relationship
WITH THE LORD

Love the Lord your God with all your heart and with all your soul and with all your mind and with all your strength.

MARK 12:30

❧

Women's ministry is exciting. There are women in every church who long for friendship, fellowship and spiritual growth. What a privilege it is to be part of a team that is helping women grow in Christ and become all that God made them to be.

The idea of women's ministry, or women ministering to women, has been around for thousands of years, as seen in Titus 2. In the everyday realities of life helping women live for Christ is becoming more and more essential in the ministry of the local church.

However, Christian service and ministry have a prerequisite—a personal relationship with Jesus Christ. This relationship is not a one-time-only event that takes place when we accept salvation but an ongoing, maturing relationship with the God who made us. Without this intimate connection to the Father, we can do nothing of eternal or lasting significance. But when we connect with Him, all things are possible in and through our very ordinary lives! Jesus speaks to His disciples about the importance of this connection in John 15. Christian ministry isn't about perfection but connection. It is through God's power that ordinary women, with ordinary circumstances

and ordinary problems, can be used for eternal purposes in His extraordinary plan.

Though ministry leaders agree that the importance of connecting with God is paramount, the busyness of life can often stifle our personal relationship with Christ and cause us to try to do things on our own and for our own purposes. Does that sound strange? Well, think about it. When we keep ourselves busy with things—even good things—our focus becomes that with which we are busy, not Jesus. It's easy to disconnect spiritually, even when we continue to serve consistently. Women's ministry is filled with details and activities, so it's easy to lose perspective. That's why we have to make sure our priorities are clear.

A LEADER'S CONNECTION

Connection is the joining of two things or the coming together of two or more people in relationship. The primary focus of a women's ministry is to provide a way for women to connect with Jesus Christ in a personal, life-changing relationship. For that to happen effectively, it must begin with the leadership. You cannot lead women somewhere you have not been. Again, this is not about activity or perfection but relationship. How can you introduce women to a relationship with Jesus if you only know Him in theory and works-based activities?

A love relationship with Jesus is not just an option for women serving other women—it is a crucial element of our walk with Christ. This is evident in the words of Christ in Revelation 2:2-5:

> I know your deeds, your hard work and your perseverance. I know that you cannot tolerate wicked men, that you have tested those who claim to be apostles but are not, and have found them false. You have persevered and have endured hardships for my name, and have not grown weary. Yet I hold this against you: You have forsaken your first love. Remember the height from which you have fallen! Repent and do the things you did at first.

Our First Love

All love relationships need to be nurtured. When we neglect our relationship with Christ, we aren't putting Him first in our life (see Matthew 6:33). How do we neglect our relationship with Him?

- By placing the emphasis on our external life rather than on our interior life (see 1 Samuel 16:7; Galatians 2:6).
- By putting other people before God and living as people pleasers (see Galatians 1:10).
- By not praying for the ministry in which we're involved (see James 5:13-18).
- By not worshiping and walking in Spirit and truth ourselves as we teach others to do so (see John 4:24).

The following personal inventory can be used by you and the other members of the women's ministry leadership team to take stock of your relationship with God at this time. It would be good to review it periodically throughout the year as you minister to others.

YOUR PERSONAL INVENTORY

First love—priority love—means giving God first place in your life.

1. On a scale of 1 to 10, how does your relationship with God rank? (**Note:** Not where a *ministry position* ranks in your life, but your personal relationship with Jesus.)

1   2   3   4   5   6   7   8   9   10
_____

Not very high   Average   Very high

2. How would you describe your present relationship with Christ?

3. Do you feel equipped to be God's vessel and to surrender all aspects of your leadership to the One who made you? If not, what do you need to do to be more prepared?

In Psalm 139:3, we see clearly that God established a relationship with David: "You discern my going out and my lying down; you are familiar with all my ways." In the same way, God is familiar with us.

In Psalm 139:23-24, David asked God to search him and to know him. David trusted God to search the deepest part of him, exposing anything that would be unhealthy to his spiritual growth. Like David, we also can have this type of relationship with God. It is a personal interaction that is not dependent on another's actions, approval or faith. It is our own personal relationship and experience with God. It is this relationship that brings glory to God.

A Daily Connection

Deuteronomy 30:19-20 outlines some directives that will help us connect with God everyday.

- **"Choose life"** (v. 19). Start each day by choosing Him (see also Joshua 24:15; Matthew 6:33).

- **"Love the Lord your God"** (v. 20). Love Him through active obedience (see also John 14:15,24; 15:10; 1 John 2:3-6).

- **"Listen to his voice"** (v. 20). Develop the habit of listening to God's voice through His Word (see also John 10:2-4; 1 Corinthians 2:14-15; Ephesians 6:17).

- **"Hold fast to him"** (v. 20). Clasp your heart around the Father's heart each day (see also Hebrews 10:35-39, 11:6, 12:1-3).

A Broken Connection

If your connection with God feels broken and you need to return to your first love, the following steps may help you to reconnect with Him:

- **Confess your sins.** Agree with God's Word and release areas of disobedience in your life (see 1 John 1:8-10).

- **Return to Him.** Make a conscious decision and an active step to follow Him (see James 4:7-10).

- **Acknowledge Him.** Turn away from human wisdom and toward God's wisdom (see Proverbs 3:5-7).

- **Praise Him.** Praise God in all things because in doing so you will catch a glimpse of His perspective, understand His power and acknowledge His divine plan (see 1 Thessalonians 5:18).

The Fruit of Connection

When Jesus manifests His power through us, that brings glory to God. The results of remaining in Christ are

- We show ourselves to be His own (see John 15:5).
- He will answer our prayers (see John 15:7,16).
- We bear much fruit (see John 15:8).
- We bring glory to the Father (see John 15:8).
- He appoints us to bear lasting fruit as His disciples (see John 15:16).

According to the *Oxford American Dictionary*, "remain" means "to continue without change; to stay after the removal or loss of others; to be left as still to be dealt with; to endure/persist."[1] To remain in Christ is serious business! We must pray for understanding and strength to continue in our relationship with Him.

The following three guidelines—the three Rs—will assist you in keeping the right perspective on what things must come first.[2]

1. Remain
How do we remain in His love? This is the key to living each day in personal relationship with the Father. We must make a conscious choice each day to stay in close fellowship with Him.

2. Renew
Romans 12:2 says "Be transformed by the renewing of your mind." Our minds should be renewed with the words of truth found in the Bible.

3. Rest
Philippians 4:6-7 tells us, "Do not be anxious about anything, but in everything, by prayer and petition, with thanksgiving, present your requests to God. And the peace of God, which transcends all understanding, will guard your hearts and your minds in Christ Jesus." According to Philippians, peace is rest!

Whenever we feel out of sorts we can use the three Rs as a check system.

- **Am I remaining today?** Have I connected in Christ and stayed connected?
- **Have I been renewed today?** Have I read and meditated on His Word today?
- **Am I resting today?** Have I prayed and turned my life and my circumstances over to God?

Often one of the Rs may be missing from our life—sometimes all of them. At that point, we need to go back to the Lord and reconnect with Him. Life boils down to one thing: a connection with God through relationship with Christ.

Before any women's ministry can be effective or bear lasting fruit, the leadership must be connected with Christ and His power. This must be the first stop, the checkpoint and the foundation for the ministry. When we put first things first, our priority becomes a love relationship of dependence on Christ and His purposes.

Notes

1. *Oxford American Dictionary,* s.v. "remain."
2. Debbie Alsdorf, *Steadfast Love* (Colorado Springs, CO: Cook Communications, 2000), p. 39.

chapter two

DISCOVERING THE *Joy* OF *Serving*

Now that I, your Lord and Teacher, have washed your feet, you also should wash one another's feet. I have set you an example that you should do as I have done for you.

JOHN 13:14-15

❧

Wash another person's feet? Sorry, but that sounds like really dirty work—not the joy of service! Yet in discovering the joy of serving others, we can find true, lasting joy and a sense of completeness.

In our selfish culture we have forgotten the beauty of serving others. It's important to understand that a very real joy can be found when we serve others, a joy that is promised by Christ Himself (see John 15:9-12).

Jesus set an example for His disciples by washing their dirty feet (see John 13:14-17). Then He told them the importance of staying connected to God for power and purpose in life. Finally, He told them that all His instructions had one purpose: That His joy would be made complete in them.

Do you long for that complete joy? We all long for joy and peace, but we usually try to obtain them the wrong way. When we serve women, we have the opportunity to bless others while sharing the joy of Jesus that is in our hearts. It's a win-win situation.

Sometimes, we just don't realize how much impact the little things can make in another's life. Read Diane's story.

Diane had a full plate. Recently, she moved to a new state; her support system of friends was a few thousand miles away; and her responsibilities included a full-time job, a husband, three teenaged children and an elderly mother to care for.

Just six months after moving to the new community, Diane's mom got sick. While she was in the hospital, Diane found her life getting much more hectic with lunch-hour check-ins and after-dinner visits to the hospital. She felt alone, tired and out of sorts.

Then one afternoon as she exited the hospital elevator, she heard laughing and chatting near her mother's room. As she rounded the corner, she realized that the laughing was actually coming from her mother's room! Her family had no personal connections in the new town. What could this be?

To her surprise, she walked into a room filled with flowers, balloons and other women. Five women from Diane's new church heard of her family's need and took over the room, baptizing every part of it with love. Just because they didn't know Diane or her mother didn't stop these women from extending love to them. The blessing of the moment brought tears to Diane's eyes.

From that point on, these women made noontime visits each day so that Diane could take a restful lunch hour and have some time alone. When Diane's mother returned home from the hospital, these women brought in meals for the first week, as Diane was busy trying to figure out her mother's new medications and all the adjustments required for her mother's care.[1]

These ordinary women knew the joy of serving others. In a very real way, they were washing feet in that hospital room and in the weeks that followed. Diane and her family never felt like strangers at church again. The service and love of five ordinary women made a tangible difference in the lives of Diane and her family.

HOW CAN I SERVE?

The first step in engaging in service is to recognize that it is part of God's plan for His people. Service is truly a God-inspired principle for living.

> Whoever wants to become great among you must be your servant, and whoever wants to be first must be your slave—just as the Son of Man did not come to be served, but to serve, and to give his life as a ransom for many (Matthew 20:26-28).

> Serve wholeheartedly, as if you were serving the Lord, not men, because you know that the Lord will reward everyone for whatever good he does (Ephesians 6:7-8).

> Whatever you do, work at it with all your heart, as working for the Lord, not for men, since you know that you will receive an inheritance from the Lord as a reward. It is the Lord Christ you are serving (Colossians 3:23-24).

WHY SERVE?

The word "serve" represents action, not inactivity. To serve means, "to work and care for, to attend, do for, minister to, wait on, to meet a need or requirement, to help."[2] How does this play out in our everyday lives?

- Christ came to serve others (see Matthew 20:28).
- We must learn to serve others (see Matthew 20:26-27).
- Serving must be done with our hearts turned toward God (see Ephesians 6:7).
- We must give our best to each act of service (see Colossians 3:23).
- No matter who we serve, we are always serving the Lord (see Colossians 3:24).
- Our reward comes from the Lord (see Ephesians 6:8; Colossians 3:24).

Everyone has daily opportunities to help someone by attending to a need or to work in someone's behalf. It can be as simple as reaching out, extending a welcome, smiling or saying hello; or it can be as complex as organizing events, setting up teams of leaders or starting a life-changing program within your local church or community. Service comes in all shapes and sizes. We all can serve, and in doing so we become more like Jesus.

HOW DOES SERVICE HELP THE LOCAL CHURCH?

In the context of women's ministry, service has broad ramifications. Women's ministries can provide a place for women to grow, develop their strengths and make lasting relationships. Because women are often more receptive to other women, a healthy women's ministry creates a climate for church growth that can affect the entire congregation. This kind of growth can reach into households, change children, affect marriages and add to the stability of people's lives. This is all possible when women are encouraged to focus on Christ as they surrender their everyday circumstances into His hands.

For service to be effective, it must start at home. That is why Scripture is very clear that women should be serving other women—and teaching them how to in turn serve their families and others.

> Then they can train the younger women to love their husbands and children, to be self-controlled and pure, to be busy at home, to be kind, and to be subject to their husbands, so that no one will malign the word of God (Titus 2:4-5).

Service is as simple as being kind, working around the house or loving those within our own four walls. Sometimes service at home can be the most difficult type of service. Remember, the joy of serving comes when we realize that we aren't merely serving people but Christ. People might forget to thank us, but Christ always blesses obedience and a heart desiring to do His will.

Obstacles

The greatest obstacles to our service are our motives and assumptions. The following are some of the most common motives and assumptions that prevent us from serving. As you read each item, ask the Lord to search your heart and reveal any struggles you may have in that area.

Self

One of the biggest obstacles in serving others is focusing our attention on ourselves and not on the power of Christ that is working through us. If we really look at ourselves, we will either give up due to feelings of inadequacy or give in to pride and self-sufficiency. Either road is disastrous.

> Such confidence as this is ours through Christ before God. Not that we are competent in ourselves to claim anything for ourselves, but our competence comes from God. He has made us competent as ministers of a new covenant—not of the letter but of the Spirit; for the letter kills, but the Spirit gives life (2 Corinthians 3:4-6).

Though we aren't always competent, we can be confident that Jesus gives us the strength to serve and minister according to His will. If we serve in faith, we will operate in a new and living way, one that gives life to those we serve. The challenge is to line ourselves up with this truth so that we have the confidence to serve.

Assumptions

It's quite easy to assume that every need is taken care of. When we have this mind-set, we also assume that our help is not necessary; therefore, we fail to serve where we are needed. God's Word makes it clear that believers operate as a functioning body, helping each other according to His plan.

> There are different kinds of gifts, but the same Spirit. There are different kinds of service, but the same Lord. There are different kinds of working, but the same God works all of them in all men. Now to each one the manifestation of the Spirit is given for the common good (1 Corinthians 12:4-7).

> The body is a unit, though it is made up of many parts; and though all its parts are many, they form one body. So it is with Christ. Now the body is not made up of one part but of many. If the foot should say, "Because I am not a hand, I do not belong to the body," it would not for that reason cease to be part of the body. The eye cannot say to the hand, "I don't need you!" And the head cannot say to the feet, "I don't need you!" (1 Corinthians 12:12,14-15,21).

As part of the Body of Christ, each of us possesses different gifts that God gave us as part of His plan. When we exercise those gifts in ministry, He provides what we lack.

Disappointment

Wherever there are people, there will be problems. God called His followers to serve one another. We will face disappointment at times, but we must lean on the Lord and maintain a standard of serving Him.

> Am I now trying to win the approval of men, or of God? Or am I trying to please men? If I were still trying to please men, I would not be a servant of Christ (Galatians 1:10).

It's important to evaluate our motives for serving by asking ourselves the difficult question: *Am I really doing this for Christ or for others?* Acknowledge that we will ultimately be disappointed in ourselves and others when we serve just for the approval of others.

Praise

It's normal to want a pat on the back and some appreciation for a job well done. However, when that's your goal, you will undoubtedly serve others for the wrong reasons. In many instances, people might not remember to thank you or even understand how hard you have worked to provide for them.

> Serve wholeheartedly, as if you were serving the Lord, not men, because you know that the Lord will reward everyone for whatever good he does (Ephesians 6:7-8).

Serving others requires us to surrender to Christ because, ultimately, we are promised a reward from God, not from man.

Time

We all wear many hats and have plenty of responsibilities to fill our days—sometimes it can be hard to find time to serve. But we must realize that our service is a choice of the heart. Once that choice is made, we can organize our lives around this goal and regularly set aside time for others.

> Each of you should look not only to your own interests, but also to the interests of others (Philippians 2:4).

Everyone has personal interests and responsibilities, but shifting our focus from ourselves to others is difficult. All changes that coincide with Scripture are possible through Christ.

Joyful Service

There is a familiar acrostic for JOY: **J**esus, **O**thers, **Y**ou. Joy comes when we put Jesus first, esteem others higher than ourselves and serve ourselves last.

> Let us not become weary in doing good, for at the proper time we will reap a harvest if we do not give up. Therefore, as we have opportunity, let us do good to all people, especially to those who belong to the family of believers (Galatians 6:9-10).

In every opportunity bless others and don't allow yourself to tire from this servant lifestyle of leadership. The Salvation Army's motto, "Heart to God—Hand to Man," perfectly explains the purpose of service. As we surrender our hearts and all that concerns us to God, He will empower us to reach out and discover what serving is all about.

Notes

1. This is a true story. Names have been changed to protect privacy.
2. *Roget's II: The New Thesaurus*, 3rd ed., s.v. "serve."

chapter three

UNCOVERING YOUR GIFTS
AND *Passion*
FOR MINISTRY

It was he who gave some to be apostles, some to be prophets, some to be evangelists, and some to be pastors and teachers, to prepare God's people for works of service, so that the body of Christ may be built up.

EPHESIANS 4:11-12

❧

God gives gifts to build up His people, not to showcase individuals. When it comes to gifts, we must remember that our talents or passions are not about us. In applying Ephesians 4:11-12 to women's ministry, we could say: Some are planners, some are hostesses and greeters, some work behind the scenes, some arrange child care, some create and decorate, some cook and serve and others deliver the message with grace.

God has prepared you for ministry since before your birth—as He told Jeremiah, "Before I formed you in the womb I knew you, before you were born I set you apart" (Jeremiah 1:5). He made your body, your personality and your temperament (see Psalm 139:13-16). Over the days, months and years of your life, circumstances have shaped and prepared you for the ministries to which He has called you. Even the very darkest moments of your life can assist you in ministering to others as you see and understand those times in light of God's plan.

In order to better understand your gifts and passions, let's take a look at your personality, your personal history and your spiritual gifts.

PERSONALITY

Your personality is the key to understanding yourself and the type of ministry that will suit you best. Gather together any group of women and you will find a very different mix of women with very different personalities! Among the people God created, there are extroverts and introverts, those who are organized and others who are organizationally challenged. There are thinkers and talkers, fireballs and peacemakers. This diversity illustrates God's design for the Body of Christ. Not everyone can do everything. Every part of the Body serves a necessary function. God created each of us for what He has prepared for us to do (see Ephesians 2:10).

Style of Ministry Indicator

The four types of personality combine to form the acrostic DISC.[1]

A woman with a D, or *driver*, personality type is a task-oriented individual who thrives on difficult assignments and wants immediate results. Her preferred work environment includes power, authority and a wide scope of operations that includes freedom from supervision. In her push to get results, she may offend more sensitive individuals. She is likely to get bored unless there are new and varied activities to challenge her. She will help your women's ministry run with a new project. Provide her with boundaries, even though she might find them uncomfortable.

Type I, the next personality type, is an *initiator*. This woman initiates contact with people and works through teams to get results. It is best to surround her with lots of people, as she thrives on fun and team spirit. She is verbal, generates enthusiasm, loves participating in a group and has a heart to help others.

S stands for *steady*. As a team member a woman with an S personality type concentrates on one task, listens well and responds to appreciation. People with steady personalities are usually very skilled in specific areas and are a great asset to a committee. Often your best craft women and decorators are of this temperament. They have the patience to see intricate tasks through to completion. To work well with her, do not rock her boat by changing something without warning. She doesn't like work to get in the way of home life, as her relationships are very important to her.

C describes the *compliant* person. A woman with a C personality type gets others to comply with her high standards, and for that reason many refer to her as being competent. She likes a clearly defined task, stability and limited risk taking. She's diplomatic and a critical thinker, and she always checks the accuracy of others. She can be assertive and competitive if combined with the *initiator* trait. When in combination with the *driver* trait, this woman can set the world on fire.

The first two temperaments are initiators: the *driver* initiates projects and the *initiator* initiates relationships with people. The second two temperaments are responders: the *steady* person responds to people, and the *compliant* person responds to projects.

The DISC temperament model lends itself to a team context, since the model focuses on personal relationships. A group of women—such as a ministry team or committee—can take the test and discuss what they discovered about themselves and how their discovery affects the group's interaction. This temperament test can also be used to place the right women in the right position in your women's ministry team. When a woman's role is consistent with her personality strength, she will actually accomplish more and be more fulfilled.

To understand your own personality strengths and weaknesses, complete the Style of Ministry Indicator and the Your Personality worksheet at the end of this chapter.

PERSONAL HISTORY

Each of us has a story. We all have experienced many events in life that form a unique personal history that God can use to encourage others. This is consistent with the biblical model of Christian interaction: sharpening, encouraging and comforting one another with the same comfort Christ gave each of us.

Don't underestimate the value of your story and how God works in your life. God's hand in your life is a miracle and an encouragement to all who see how God deals with you personally.

Your passion for a certain type of service will probably develop through something you've experienced or through areas in which you've discovered a need for God. In other words, the areas in your life in which you've felt weak and later received strength will most likely become the areas about which you are passionate when interacting with others.

Often, personal history can dictate your passions or shape your ability to serve with purpose. Consider Rosa's story:

Rosa appeared to be raising the perfect Christian family. Her three children attended Christian school, she and her husband served at church, and everything in life was stable. Then her daughter, Lynn, graduated from high school.

Lynn enrolled at a junior college and quickly got involved with the wrong group. It wasn't long before alcohol and marijuana became part of Lynn's life. About a year later, the dreaded call came: Lynn had been in an accident—she and another young person were killed. Lynn's death devastated Rosa's family.

After a time of healing, Rosa found herself drawn to any news or magazine article she came across about wayward teens and alcohol abuse. A few years down the road, she started an organization in her community to help the parents of wayward teens. How could she do this after losing her own daughter? She did it because her personal history gave her an intense interest in the subject and a heart-felt passion to help in any way she could. Through prayer and God's guidance, she sought to provide for others everything she wished had been available for her.[2]

To better understand your own personal history and the impact it can have on your area of service, complete the Personal History Inventory at the end of this chapter. Prayerfully ask God to show you areas in which you might serve others based on your own experiences.

SPIRITUAL GIFTS

Spiritual gifts indicate what you may do when serving others. Just as the body has many parts, so the Body of Christ is made up of different people, each with his or her own personality, personal history and gifts. It isn't necessary to have the spiritual gift of leadership to become an effective leader. The Bible often refers to leading people as shepherding, which involves encouragement, exhortation and the ability to give guidance or direction.[3]

Some people are well suited to public ministry while others prefer more intimate, small group settings. Those who lead larger groups tend toward a prophetic type of leadership—casting vision and proclaiming truth—and may not be effective small-group leaders. Those who have strong relational skills and a desire to shepherd others through building relationships are probably best suited for leading small groups.

The following glossary of spiritual gifts is taken from *Discover Your Spiritual Gifts* by C. Peter Wagner. The book contains additional information and a questionnaire to aid you in discovering your own spiritual gifts. If you would like to order *Discover Your Spiritual Gifts* or the self-scoring *Finding Your Spiritual Gifts* inventory, please call your Christian supplier or contact Gospel Light at 1-800-4-GOSPEL or www.gospellight.com.

Glossary of Spiritual Gifts

Administration: The special ability to understand clearly the immediate and long-range goals of a particular unit of the Body and to devise and execute effective plans for the accomplishment of those goals (see Luke 14:28-30; Acts 6:1-7; 27:11; 1 Cor. 12:28; Titus 1:5).

Apostle: The special ability to assume and exercise general leadership within God-assigned spheres such as ecclesiastical, territorial, functional, marketplace, etc., accompanied by an extraordinary authority in spiritual matters that is spontaneously recognized and appreciated by those within the sphere (see 1 Cor. 12:28; Eph. 2:20; 4:11).

Celibacy: The special ability to remain single and enjoy it and not suffer undue sexual temptations (see Matt. 19:10-12; 1 Cor. 7:7-8).

Deliverance: The special ability to cast out demons and evil spirits (see Matt. 12:22-32; Luke 10:12-20; Acts 8:5-8; 16:16-18).

Discerning of spirits: The special ability to know with assurance whether certain behaviors purported to be of God are in reality divine, human or satanic (see Matt. 16:21-23; Acts 5:1-11; 16:16-18; 1 Cor. 12:10; 1 John 4:1-6).

Evangelist: The special ability to share the gospel with unbelievers in such a way that men and women become Jesus' disciples and responsible members of the Body of Christ (see Acts 8:5-6,26-40; 14:21; 21:8; Eph. 4:11-14; 2 Tim. 4:5).

Exhortation: The special ability to minister words of comfort, consolation, encouragement and counsel to other members of the Body in such a way that they feel helped and healed (see Acts 14:22; Rom. 12:8; 1 Tim. 4:13; Heb. 10:25).

Faith: The special ability to discern with extraordinary confidence the will and purposes of God for the future of His work (see Acts 11:22-24; 27:21-25; Rom. 4:18-21; 1 Cor. 12:9; Heb. 11).

Giving: The special ability to contribute material resources to the work of the Lord with liberality and cheerfulness (see Mark 12:41-44; Rom. 12:8; 2 Cor. 8:1-7; 9:2-8).

Healing: The special ability to serve as human intermediaries through whom it pleases God to cure illness and restore health apart from the use of natural means (see Acts 3:1-10; 5:12-16; 9:32-35; 28:7-10; 1 Cor. 12:9,28).

Helps: The special ability to invest their talents in the life and ministry of other members of the Body, most frequently leaders, thus enabling the leader to increase the effectiveness of his or her spiritual gifts (see Mark 15:40-41; Luke 8:2-3; Acts 9:36; Rom. 16:1-2; 1 Cor. 12:28).

Hospitality: The special ability to provide open house and warm welcome for those in need of food and lodging (see Acts 16:14-15; Rom. 12:9-13; Rom. 16:23; Heb. 13:1-2; 1 Pet. 4:9).

Intercession: The special ability to pray for extended periods of time on a regular basis and see frequent and specific answers to their prayers to a degree much greater than that which is expected of the average Christian (see Luke 22:41-44; Acts 12:12; Col. 1:9-12; 4:12-13; 1 Tim. 2:1-2; Jas. 5:14-16).

Interpretation of tongues: The special ability to make known in the vernacular the message of one who speaks in tongues (see 1 Cor. 12:10,30; 14:13-14,26-28).

Knowledge: The special ability to discover, accumulate, analyze and clarify information and ideas that are pertinent to the growth and well-being of the Body (see Acts 5:1-11; 1 Cor. 2:14; 12:8; 2 Cor. 11:6; Col. 2:2-3).

Leadership: The special ability to set goals in accordance with God's purpose for the future and to communicate these goals to others in such a way that they voluntarily and harmoniously work together to accomplish those goals for the glory of God (see Luke 9:51; Acts 7:10; 15:7-11; Romans 12:8; 1 Tim. 5:17; Heb. 13:17).

Leading worship: The special ability to usher a congregation into the presence of God through music, prayer, dance and other visual forms (see 1 Sam 16:23; 1 Chron. 9:33; Ps. 34:3).

Martyrdom: The special ability to undergo suffering for the faith even to death while consistently displaying a joyous and victorious attitude that brings glory to God (see Acts 22:20; 1 Cor. 13:3; Rev. 2:13; 17:6).

Mercy: The special ability to feel genuine empathy and compassion for individuals, both Christian and non-Christian, who suffer distressing physical, mental or emotional problems, and to translate that compassion into cheerfully done deeds that reflect Christ's love and alleviate suffering (see Matt. 20:29-34; 25:34-40; Mark 9:41; Luke 10:33-35; Acts 11:28-30; 16:33-34; Rom. 12:8).

Miracles: The special ability to serve as human intermediaries through whom it pleases God to perform powerful acts that are perceived by observers to have altered the ordinary course of nature (see Acts 9:36-42; 19:11-20; 20:7-12; Rom. 15:18-19; 1 Cor. 12:10,28; 2 Cor. 12:12).

Missionary: The special ability to minister in another culture (see Acts 8:4; 13:2-3; 22:21; Rom. 10:15; 1 Cor. 9:19-23).

Pastor: The special ability to assume a long-term personal responsibility for the spiritual welfare of a group of believers (see John 10:1-18; Eph. 4:11-14; 1 Tim. 3:1-7; 1 Pet. 5:1-3).

Prophecy: The special ability to receive and communicate an immediate message of God to His people through a divinely anointed utterance (see Luke 7:26; Acts 15:32; Acts 21:9-11; Rom. 12:6; 1 Cor. 12:10,28; Eph. 4:11-13).

Service: The special ability to identify the unmet needs involved in a task related to God's work and to make use of available resources to meet those needs and help accomplish the desired goals (see Acts 6:1-7; Rom. 12:7; Gal. 6:2,10; 2 Tim. 1:16-18; Titus 3:14).

Teaching: The special ability to communicate information relevant to the health and ministry of the Body and its members in such a way that others will learn (see Acts 18:24-28; 20:20-21; Rom. 12:7; 1 Cor. 12:28; Eph. 4:11-14).

Tongues: The special ability (1) to speak to God in a language they have never learned and/or (2) to receive and communicate an immediate message from God to His people through a divinely anointed utterance in a language they have never learned (see Mark 16:17; Acts 2:1-13; 10:44-46; 19:1-7; 1 Cor. 12:10, 28; 14:13-19).

Voluntary poverty: The special ability to serve God more effectively by renouncing material comfort and luxury and adopting a personal lifestyle equivalent to those living at the poverty level in a given society (see Acts 2:44-45; 4:34-37; 1 Cor. 13:1-3; 2 Cor. 6:10; 8:9).

Wisdom: The special ability to know the mind of the Holy Spirit in such a way as to receive insight into how given knowledge may best be applied to specific needs arising in the Body of Christ (see Acts 6:3,10; 1 Cor. 2:1-13; 12:8; Jas. 1:5-6; 2 Pet. 3:15-16).[4]

BIBLICAL LEADERSHIP

The most important thing a leader must possess is a personal relationship with Christ. Only then can God work through personality, personal history and spiritual gifts. They must also live with passion for Christ and desire to finish the race with integrity.

Qualifications of Leadership

Christ Follower—Having a Passion for Christ
- Turn from sin in your life (see 1 John 1:9; Romans 6:6).
- Read God's Word and pray (see Colossians 3:16; 1 Peter 2:2).
- Be filled with the Spirit (see Romans 7:6; Ephesians 5:18).
- Use your gifts in ministry (see Romans 12:3-8; 1 Peter 4:10-11).
- Learn to persevere in the face of adversity (see Romans 5:3-5; Philippians 1:29; 1 Peter 4:12-14).

Character—Paying Attention to the Heart
- Be transformed in the image of Christ instead of conformed to the world. (see Romans 8:28-30; 12:1-2; Philippians 1:9-10).
- Develop a character worthy of leadership (see 1 Thessalonians 1:3; 1 Timothy 3:1-15; Titus 1:5-9).

Calling—Called to Shepherd God's People
- See others with the compassion of Christ (see Matthew 9:36-38).
- Allow yourself to be moved by the needs of others; and care for them (see Philippians 1:8; 1 Thessalonians 2:7-8; 1 Peter 5:1-4).

Commitment—Doing What It Takes
- Realize that leadership is based on commitment, not convenience (see John 13:12-17).
- Leaders are committed to seeing their followers grow in Christ (see Matthew 28:18-20; 2 Timothy 2:2).

When we understand that God desires to use each of us for the edification of others, something begins to grow within us. Passion begins to fuel all that we do in our service to Christ and others.[5]

When you serve other women by using your gifts for the overall good, you will develop a great enthusiasm and passion. By focusing on Christ, you will discover your gifts, heed your calling and live with the passion that only the Spirit of Christ can give you. In the book *Leading Life-Changing Small Groups*, J. Oswald Sanders was quoted as saying:

Reduced to its simplest terms, to be filled with the Spirit means that, through voluntary surrender and in response to appropriating faith, the human personality is filled, mastered, controlled by the Holy Spirit.[6]

It is hoped that you will take the information you have gleaned from these inventories to make sure that you and your leadership council members are serving in the areas and ministries that are a match for your personalities, gifts, passions and abilities.

Celebrate the differences within your group, and use them for the glory of God!

Notes

1. Carol Porter and Mike Hamel, eds., *The Women's Ministry Handbook*, (Colorado Springs, CO: Chariot Victor Books, 1992), p. 32.
2. This is a true story. Names have been changed to protect privacy.
3. Bill Donahue, *Leading Life-Changing Small Groups*, rev. ed. (Grand Rapids, MI: Zondervan Publishing House, 1996), p. 61.
4. C. Peter Wagner, *Discover Your Spiritual Gifts* (Ventura, CA: Regal Books, 2002), pp. 91-95. Used by permission.
5. Donahue, *Leading Life-Changing Small Groups*, rev. ed., p. 39.
6. J. Oswald Sanders, quoted in Bill Donahue, *Leading Life-Changing Small Groups*, rev. ed. (Grand Rapids, MI: Zondervan Publishing House, 1996), p. 59.

STYLE OF MINISTRY INDICATOR

Directions: In each of the following rows of four words, place a check in the box in front of the one word that most often applies to you. If there are two words that both clearly describe you, then mark them both, but select no more than two. If you reach a row of words that does not describe you at all, then skip that row. After completing the sheet, add up all the check marks in each of the four columns.

Strengths

1.	☐ Adventurous	☐ Animated	☐ Adaptable	☐ Analytical
2.	☐ Persuasive	☐ Playful	☐ Peaceful	☐ Persistent
3.	☐ Strong-willed	☐ Sociable	☐ Submissive	☐ Self-sacrificing
4.	☐ Competitive	☐ Convincing	☐ Controlled	☐ Considerate
5.	☐ Resourceful	☐ Refreshing	☐ Reserved	☐ Respectful
6.	☐ Self-reliant	☐ Spirited	☐ Satisfied	☐ Sensitive
7.	☐ Positive	☐ Promoter	☐ Patient	☐ Planner
8.	☐ Sure	☐ Spontaneous	☐ Shy	☐ Scheduled
9.	☐ Outspoken	☐ Optimistic	☐ Obliging	☐ Orderly
10.	☐ Forceful	☐ Funny	☐ Friendly	☐ Faithful
11.	☐ Daring	☐ Delightful	☐ Diplomatic	☐ Detailed
12.	☐ Confident	☐ Cheerful	☐ Consistent	☐ Cultured
13.	☐ Independent	☐ Inspiring	☐ Inoffensive	☐ Idealistic
14.	☐ Decisive	☐ Demonstrative	☐ Dry humor	☐ Deep
15.	☐ Mover	☐ Mixes easily	☐ Mediator	☐ Musical
16.	☐ Tenacious	☐ Talker	☐ Tolerant	☐ Thoughtful
17.	☐ Leader	☐ Lively	☐ Listener	☐ Loyal
18.	☐ Chief	☐ Cute	☐ Contented	☐ Chart maker
19.	☐ Productive	☐ Popular	☐ Permissive	☐ Perfectionist
20.	☐ Bold	☐ Bouncy	☐ Balanced	☐ Behaved

Weaknesses

21.	☐ Bossy	☐ Brassy	☐ Blank	☐ Bashful
22.	☐ Unsympathetic	☐ Undisciplined	☐ Unenthusiastic	☐ Unforgiving
23.	☐ Resistant	☐ Repetitious	☐ Reticent	☐ Resentful
24.	☐ Frank	☐ Forgetful	☐ Fearful	☐ Fussy
25.	☐ Impatient	☐ Interrupts	☐ Indecisive	☐ Insecure
26.	☐ Unaffectionate	☐ Unpredictable	☐ Uninvolved	☐ Unpopular
27.	☐ Headstrong	☐ Haphazard	☐ Hesitant	☐ Hard-to-please
28.	☐ Proud	☐ Permissive	☐ Plain	☐ Pessimistic
29.	☐ Argumentative	☐ Angered easily	☐ Aimless	☐ Alienated
30.	☐ Nervy	☐ Naive	☐ Nonchalant	☐ Negative attitude
31.	☐ Workaholic	☐ Wants credit	☐ Worrier	☐ Withdrawn
32.	☐ Tactless	☐ Talkative	☐ Timid	☐ Too sensitive

33.	❑ Domineering	❑ Disorganized	❑ Doubtful	❑ Depressed
34.	❑ Intolerant	❑ Inconsistent	❑ Indifferent	❑ Introvert
35.	❑ Manipulative	❑ Messy	❑ Mumbles	❑ Moody
36.	❑ Stubborn	❑ Show-off	❑ Slow	❑ Skeptical
37.	❑ Lord-over-others	❑ Loud	❑ Lazy	❑ Loner
38.	❑ Short-tempered	❑ Scatter-brained	❑ Sluggish	❑ Suspicious
39.	❑ Rash	❑ Restless	❑ Reluctant	❑ Revengeful
40.	❑ Crafty	❑ Changeable	❑ Compromising	❑ Critical

Totals _____ **Driver** _____ **Initiator** _____ **Steady** _____ **Compliant**[1]

1. Carol Porter and Mike Hamel, eds., *The Women's Ministry Handbook* (Colorado Springs, CO: Chariot Victor Books, 1992), p. 39.

Y O U R
P E R S O N A L I T Y

When it comes to your personal style there is no right or wrong. Ask yourself the following questions to help you define how God made you, and how you have developed as a person.

1. What makes you laugh?

2. What energizes you?

3. What encourages you?

4. What interests you?

5. What do you enjoy doing in your spare time?

6. What brings you peace?

7. What brings you the most happiness?

8. Do you like small or large crowds?

9. Are you an up-front or behind-the-scenes-type person?

10. Are you creative or administrative?

11. Based on the DISC explanation and your answers to the above questions, summarize who you are in the context of a women's ministry team. Be as specific as you can.

PERSONAL HISTORY INVENTORY

Personal history can indicate an area in which you are well suited to serve. In the following section, check all areas that have affected your life in some way.

- ❑ Abuse
- ❑ Adoption
- ❑ Alcoholism or addiction
- ❑ Blended family issues
- ❑ Empty nest
- ❑ Cancer survivor
- ❑ Death of a child
- ❑ Death of a spouse
- ❑ Dissatisfaction with job
- ❑ Eating disorder
- ❑ Fertility issues
- ❑ Husband who travels a lot
- ❑ Loss of a close friendship
- ❑ Loss of marriage romance
- ❑ Major change in health
- ❑ Miscarriage
- ❑ Problems with teens
- ❑ Retirement
- ❑ Infant death
- ❑ Taking care of older parents
- ❑ Unwanted pregnancy

- ❑ Abortion
- ❑ AIDS
- ❑ Aging issues
- ❑ Children who have special needs
- ❑ Chronic fatigue
- ❑ Chronic illness or injury
- ❑ Death of a parent
- ❑ Depression or mental illness
- ❑ Divorce or separation
- ❑ Fear/anxiety/panic
- ❑ Husband who is not a believer
- ❑ Loneliness
- ❑ Loss of a job
- ❑ Low self-esteem
- ❑ Major change in residence
- ❑ Pregnancy
- ❑ Remaining single
- ❑ Stillborn baby
- ❑ Suicide or attempted suicide
- ❑ Trouble with in-laws

- ❑ Any other incident that stands out in your personal history:

PASSION ASSESSMENT

Directions

- Prayerfully consider your answers to the following questions.
- Complete the following assessment on your own.
- Remember, there are no right or wrong responses.
- Don't be concerned about whether you think you can do it or how it would be done.
- Complete the assessment as if you have no obstacles to fulfilling your heart's desire.

1. If you knew that you couldn't fail and money were no object, what would you do?

2. At the end of your life, what would you love to be able to look back on and know you had done something about?

3. If someone were to mention your name to a group of your friends, what would your friends say you are really interested in or passionate about?

4. What topics would keep you talking late into the night?

5. What would you most like to do for others?

6. Which group would you most like to help?

- ❑ Career women
- ❑ College students
- ❑ Divorcees
- ❑ Empty nesters
- ❑ The hospitalized
- ❑ Parents
- ❑ Prisoners
- ❑ Single parents
- ❑ Teen mothers
- ❑ Widows
- ❑ Youth
- ❑ Other:
- ❑ Children
- ❑ The disabled
- ❑ The elderly
- ❑ The homeless
- ❑ Infants
- ❑ The poor
- ❑ Refugees
- ❑ Singles
- ❑ The unemployed
- ❑ Young married couples

7. About which issues or causes do you feel strongly?

- ❑ Abortion
- ❑ AIDS
- ❑ Church
- ❑ Economy
- ❑ Environment
- ❑ Foreign born
- ❑ Homosexuality
- ❑ Injustice
- ❑ Politics
- ❑ Racism
- ❑ Technology
- ❑ Other:
- ❑ Addictions
- ❑ Child care
- ❑ Discipleship
- ❑ Education
- ❑ Family
- ❑ Health care
- ❑ Hunger
- ❑ Literacy
- ❑ Poverty
- ❑ Reaching unbelievers
- ❑ Violence

8. List five to seven of the most positive experiences you've had in your life and briefly describe what you did and why each experience was meaningful:

9. In what area(s) from questions 6 and 7 do you think you could make the most significant contribution?

10. Based on your answers to the these questions, where do you sense your passions lie?*

* Bruce Bugbee, Don Cousins and Bill Hybels, *Network* (Grand Rapids, MI: Zondervan Publishing House, 1994), pp. 15-16.

STARTING
THE *Ministry*

chapter four

STARTING A WOMEN'S *Ministry*

Unless the LORD builds the house, its builders labor in vain.

PSALM 127:1

❧

The basic goal of women's ministry is to gather women together for the purpose of sharing the life of Christ with them and through them. A women's ministry is not a club or an exclusive sorority; its purpose is to provide the building tools needed for each woman to reach deep into her heart so that she might be built up into what God called and purposed her to be. Because a women's ministry is so much more than a women's group, it is vital to seek God's intention, direction and vision from the beginning—and every step along the way.

WHY MINISTER SPECIFICALLY TO WOMEN?

God created women to be more relationally oriented than men; we thrive when our relationships thrive. Prior to the 1970s, women nurtured and befriended the women in their families and communities, which met their unique relational needs. However, in today's culture a woman often finds herself isolated from other women whether she is single, a stay-at-home mom or career-oriented. The Church has a golden opportunity to minister to the relational needs of women by providing meeting opportunities for Christ-centered fellowship and spiritual growth.

Take a look at the following statistics about women in the Church:

- 60 percent of church attendees are women.
- 90 percent of American women consider themselves "Christians."
- Women are twice as likely to be involved in a discipleship program than men and are more likely to be involved in a small group than men.
- Women are more likely to hold a leadership position in the church than men.
- Women are more likely to disciple others than men.
- 24 percent of women performed some type of volunteer work at their church in the last week.[1]

Research shows that women are an integral part of the daily life of the Church. They are some of the primary volunteers, leaders and mentors. As women, we also face personal challenges that make it hard to keep our heads above water and our priorities in check.

How do the following sayings illustrate a woman's uniqueness?

- A woman's work is never done.

- The hand that rocks the cradle rules the world.
- If Mama's not happy, ain't nobody happy.
- The man is the head of the home, but the woman is the heart.
- A woman sets the temperature and her rhythm regulates the heartbeat of the home.
- "A quarrelsome wife is like a constant dripping on a rainy day" (Proverbs 27:15).
- "Train the younger women to love their husbands and children" (Titus 2:4).

In order to improve the spiritual health of the Church, it is imperative to improve the spiritual vitality of the women within it.

GETTING STARTED

Jill Briscoe, a seasoned women's ministry leader, said, "The best way to begin is to begin." She wrote about her early excuses:

> The first thing I discovered about working with women was that I was one! Now that isn't a facetious remark, either. Believing I could never serve women because I didn't understand their needs was a trick the devil had played on me. That had only been an excuse. All I had to do was figure out my needs and how God could meet them and then learn how to press the need button for other women as well. Secondly I learned that if I was going to work with women, I would never run out of material. Half the human race were women! Women were everywhere.[2]

Women are indeed everywhere. If you want to develop a women's ministry within your church, you are probably excited about the possibilities and, maybe, a bit overwhelmed by the responsibility. So how do you start a ministry within your local church?

First, begin talking to others about the idea. Let people know you would like to see a women's ministry in your church. Identify others who have a similar interest. Ask the pastor's wife if she has any interest in beginning a women's ministry, and if not, ask her if she has any suggestions for you that she has gleaned from other churches.

Next, invite a small group of interested women to talk about what the women in your church need. Then brainstorm how to meet those needs.

Put together an informal proposal of what a women's ministry would look like at your church, and arrange a meeting with the pastor for prayer and advice. Be realistic in your preliminary plan; consider the needs as well as the abilities of the women at your church.

Note: Always submit yourself to the authority that God has placed over your family and the church, such as your husband or church pastoral staff.

BUILDING A PROPER FOUNDATION

There are endless activities you can plan for the women in your church and community, but the basis of your women's ministry needs to be on studying and applying God's Word. The first order of business for any women's ministry is to set up a women's Bible study. As you work Bible study into the agenda, you will need to develop a team to establish the ministry's foundation.

Once your pastoral leadership gives you the green light, form a team of women who are interested in working from the ground up: survey the women in the church, develop a purpose statement and define the leadership structure. This team will also clarify the primary purpose of the women's ministry for your church, discover the needs of the women in your church and community and brainstorm ideas to meet those needs.

If you are starting from scratch, you might announce a meeting for those interested in the planning of a women's ministry. Ask God for a small group of ministry-minded, godly women who will help lay the foundation. These women may eventually become leaders, or the Lord may have placed them there only to act as the initial steering committee.

ORGANIZING FROM THE INSIDE OUT

Organization frees us and enables us to do God's will. Organization does not chip away at the Holy Spirit's work or replace the Spirit's prompting, but it facilitates the ministry that He has inspired within your heart.

Organizational needs differ depending on the size of the church. In a small church of 50 to 100 people, very little organization is needed to develop relationships. Most women in a small church already know each other and may meet together for prayer, study and fellowship. These meetings are easily arranged through bulletin announcements or phone calls. But even in a small church, the women's ministry needs leadership to fulfill its vision and purpose.

A large church presents a variety of ever-changing needs, as the members comprise diverse backgrounds, life circumstances, ages and interests. The more people involved in a ministry, the more vital organization becomes. The need for organization rises with each new person who attends your church.

To build an effective ministry, leaders must develop in the following areas:

- Time management
- Goal setting
- Priority planning
- Relationship building

Not any one person will necessarily have all of these skills mastered. Each woman will bring her own strengths and skills to the team and team members can learn the skills needed from one another.

Time Management

Without a purpose we all wander aimlessly. Many people live from day to day just surviving! Survival is good, but fulfilling a purpose is better. An essential part of a thriving ministry is to make the most of the hours God gives us.

Consider Donna's story:

When Donna was a young mother of three children, all she could do was just get through each day. She had no real plan and little reason for doing any activity at a specific time of day. Each day took on a familiar boring atmosphere and she felt stuck in the ordinary rut. She watched other women serve and marveled at how they seemed to be able to manage their families while serving God. She desperately wanted to find time to use her gifts and serve God too.

Donna was struck by the fact that she could manage her time better if she really wanted to. If all of her life was to belong to God, then her time was no exception. He wanted to bring into her life people who needed Him as Savior or who needed help or encouragement. To have time for ministry, she had to identify what was important in her life and then take the necessary steps to make those things a reality.

The first step, as simplistic as it sounds, was getting a wall calendar that stayed in one spot in her home. She also found a day planner that fit into her purse. With these tools she began organizing her life around her family schedule and church commitments. Next she learned to organize her daily responsibilities by prioritizing them. Each day she had certain responsibilities that had to be done, regardless of how she felt about doing those tasks. Before long her life seemed to take shape, and she was no longer looking out of a window at people who could manage a busy, fulfilling life— she was one of them.

With her family taken care of and a calendar in hand, she was able to determine the amount of time she could designate to ministry at her local church, volunteer hours at the local school and social time that encouraged her to be more hospitable.

She had tried calendars, lists and schedules before, but really using the calendar and really doing what she had committed to do each day made the difference this time. This lifestyle change was hard at first, but with time and repetition it became part of her life.

What also became part of her life was a more purposeful time for study, prayer and spiritual development. No longer living aimlessly, she actually had more time than she had previously thought. As a result, peace began to flood her soul, and daily surrender to God's plan—His day planner for her—began to take on new meaning and started to unfold in an exciting adventure. It all started with a choice to turn this area of her life around. And that choice is influencing her life with Christ each new day.[3]

Everyone has 24 hours in each day. How we choose to use that time determines what gets done. Understanding that our time belongs to God enables us to surrender our time for His use and keeps us from getting overwhelmed or becoming works oriented.

Christ's Example

Though not called time management in His day, Jesus set an example of surrender, sacrifice and making wise use of the time given to Him.

- He made time for being alone (see Mark 1:35).
- He made time for prayer (see Matthew 14:23).
- He made time for teaching (see Matthew 5:1-2).
- He made time for ministry (see John 13:1-17).

Goal Setting

Your goals will determine the direction of your ministry and your life. You can be like the person James describes as "like a wave of the sea, blown and tossed by the wind . . . double-minded . . . unstable in all he does" (James 1:6,8), or you can set your sail so that the ship of your life catches the wind of the Holy Spirit!

If you're going to reach your goals, they must be measurable and realistic. First consider the time frame for reaching your goals. Without a specific length of time against which to check your progress, it's unlikely that you'll make any progress. Clearly state each goal and decide how you will accomplish it, or come closer to it, in a week's or month's time.

Have you developed a personal mission statement? What do you want to accomplish in your time here on Earth? Your personal mission statement should help define your goals. Since goals determine the course we take, they play a part in the legacy we leave behind. What do you want people to remember about you? What about your life do you want people to remember when you're gone? Answering such questions helps determine the short- and long-term goals you need to set to accomplish that legacy. You can use your personal mission statement to periodically check your progress against the bigger picture. Remember, if you don't have a sense of direction, you won't be able to lead others!

Luke 2:52 gives us a framework when considering goals: "Jesus grew in wisdom and stature, and in favor with God and men." This passage illustrates growth in four areas: intellectual, physical, spiritual and social. For each of those categories, take a moment to write down a few personal goals.

- Intellectual—*Growing in wisdom*

- Physical—*Growing in stature*

- Spiritual—*Growing in favor with God*

· Social—*Growing in favor with people*

Priority Planning

When seeking to establish new priorities, organizational skills become an important part of the picture. There are many ways to improve your prioritizing skills. The following are some helpful steps to becoming more organized:

- Prayerfully plan the day's activities the night before or early in the morning.
- Remember the 80/20 principle: 80 percent of the job is done in the first 20 percent of the time it takes to complete a project.
- Make a list of the day's tasks and activities. Assign each task an A, B or C ranking, with A being the top priority. Delegate as many C items as possible to others.
- Carry a calendar, notebook or personal digital assistant (PDA), and use it!
- Keep one weekly to-do list. This list can replace those messy sticky notes or scraps of paper!
- Watch your phone time. Screen calls and return them when it fits your schedule.
- Get exercise! Your energy level will soar if you are physically active. Raising your serotonin levels through exercise causes your stress levels to decrease. Make exercise a priority.
- Put relaxation days on your calendar. Remember the Sabbath? You need rest away from ministry, people and work.
- Organize your house and/or workspace to relieve stress.
- Create a weekly or monthly menu plan. Preparing ahead in this area will relieve the stress of having to make decisions in the evening hours.

Relationship Building

To be involved in women's ministry, you have to be involved with women. Some women are overly sensitive and easily hurt. Though hurt feelings can't be avoided, relationships and people are important. Each person is of great worth and value to God—worth your extra effort. Each woman needs to grow, and God can use others as mirrors and sharpening tools.

Your key leadership team must be united in purpose, passion and vision. To accomplish this amazing feat, a few key elements should be in place:

- Loyalty to God
- Loyalty to His Word
- Loyalty to His people
- Loyalty to one another

The dictionary defines "loyal" as, "steadfast in one's allegiance to a person."[4] Allegiance to another person is a by-product of healthy relationships. One goal of your women's ministry should be to build relationships that are centered on biblical truth, commitment to Christ and allegiance to one another.

Special events should not be limited to the women reached by the ministry—plan special events for the leadership team as well. These leadership events will go further than you can imagine in fostering an effective team of leaders! The following are some quick ideas for quality, fun, get-to-know-you times.

Leadership Retreat

Pick a spot for a weekend get-together. Have the key leaders plan a direction for the retreat's teaching. Keep it personable and intimate as women study the Word and fellowship together. Have a few leaders share their personal testimonies with the other leaders in this intimate setting. Be prepared to bond. Include some fun activities to encourage laughter—a great team builder.

Leadership Spa Day

This could be a little pricey if you go to a real spa, but what a treat! If it's out of the question due to budget, get together at a leader's home and make your own retreat—hot tub, manicures, pedicures, facials and other girl stuff. There's something about seeing each other without makeup that really bonds a group!

Leadership Tea

Don't reserve the pretty stuff for the entire group; invite the leadership team over and have an elegant tea party. End the tea by sharing prayer requests and supporting one another.

Leadership Sleepover

The little girls do it, the youth group does it—why shouldn't we? Pick a house, rent some "chick flick" videos, munch on snacks and let the little girl in each of you come out and play. This could be a fun way to close out a ministry year—a time for the leadership team to relax and enjoy the fruits of their service.

You get the idea—anything that gets your team together in a different setting to laugh and relax will work.

Notes

1. "Women Are the Backbone of the Christian Congregations in America," March 6, 2000, *The Barna Group.* http://www.barna.org/FlexPage.aspx?Page=BarnaUpdate&BarnaUpdateID=47 (accessed May 11, 2004).
2. Jill Briscoe, *Designing Effective Women's Ministries,* (Grand Rapids, MI: Zondervan Publishing House, 1995), p. 17.
3. This is a true story. Names have been changed to protect privacy.
4. *Oxford American Dictionary,* s.v. "loyal."

chapter five

Developing a
PURPOSE, VISION AND MISSION

Where there is no vision, the people perish.

PROVERBS 29:18 (KJV)

The word translated as "perish" in this verse in the *King James Version* of the Bible is translated in the *New International Version* as "unrestrained," meaning people can't focus, can't reach their goal, can't follow their dream. Bill Hybels, pastor of Willow Creek Community Church said,

> I have seen it with my own eyes—without vision, people lose the vitality that makes them feel alive.
>
> In the 1940s a young evangelist named Billy Graham had a radical dream. He and a few college buddies envisioned packed stadiums where people far from God could hear the proclamation of the gospel. As of this year, 210 million people have heard Billy Graham preach live, while over one billion have heard Dr. Graham present the gospel via television and radio. [1]

What do you envision happening to the women in your church and in your community? What do you imagine when thinking about changing the lives of women, or helping them becoming all that God called them to be?

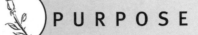

PURPOSE

Before organizing any ministry, you need to pinpoint and clarify your purpose. This purpose statement should be your compass as the ministry develops.

Elmbrook Church, in Brookfield, Wisconsin, is noted for many things, including an outstanding women's ministry. Though it is a larger church than most women's ministries will ever encounter, its ideas are helpful to any sized group. In the book *Designing Effective Women's Ministries*, the authors discuss the ministry's purpose statement:

> Hammering out a purpose statement is not difficult. You might want to invite either a leadership team or all the women interested in women's ministries in your church to a purpose statement brainstorming session. Ask each woman to bring along a one-sentence statement of what she believes is or should be the purpose of the women's ministries. At the session divide the women into groups of three or four and allow time for small group prayer for God's leadership and unity. Then ask the women to share their prepared sentences with their small groups. Allow twenty minutes for each group to consolidate their ideas and agree upon a one-sentence purpose statement. Bringing all the small groups back together again, have each small group share theirs aloud, and write

these on the board or overhead for all to see. Then as a large group, formulate a one or two sentence statement which describes the intent of your ministry.[2]

Here is the purpose statement created for Elmbrook:

The Elmbrook Church Women's Ministries emphasize women ministering to women for the purpose of encouraging, equipping and evangelizing women in Milwaukee, the Midwest, the United States and across the globe.[3]

Does your church have a clearly stated purpose? If so, then start there when developing a purpose for your women's ministry. If a church has as its purpose: "To exalt the Lord, to evangelize the community, to edify and equip the believer," then the women's ministry in that church should embody these same goals.

When determining a purpose statement, keep in mind the purpose of the church at large. At Cornerstone Fellowship in Livermore, California, the women's ministry reflects the same mission and purpose of the church. The church's purpose statement is

Cornerstone Fellowship exists to reach people with the love of Jesus; connect them to the community of believers; grow them toward spiritual maturity while they serve others, and worship God.[4]

Its women's ministry's purpose statement is "Cornerstone women's ministry exists to connect women to God and to each other."[5]

These statements are united in intent and purpose. The shorter women's statement still embodies the key elements of the church statement: reach, connect, grow, serve and worship.

Getting Started

A clear purpose is the bedrock upon which all ministries are planned and established. So the first goal of a new women's ministry leadership team would be to establish the purpose of that women's ministry.

Here is how to get started.

- Begin with prayer.
- Every woman on the team should give her input.
- All input must be considered.
- Evaluate against the general church purpose.
- Write down each suggested purpose.
- Fine tune the wording. Check grammar, and make sure the wording flows easily.
- Pray through each step of the process.

A purpose statement should reflect a balanced program. Include both inreach and outreach as essential elements to a healthy women's ministry. The purpose statement acts as a compass providing a direction for your ministry and your ministry events. If you know what you want to accomplish, then programs and ideas can be evaluated and determined by your purpose statement.

Your ministry's purpose statement needs to be periodically reevaluated and revised as the needs of your ministry change. It's important that the statement accurately reflects your ministry.

- Have you defined the purpose of your women's ministry and designed a purpose statement?
- Has your purpose been communicated to the women in your ministry?
- Were your women's ministry leaders involved in the designing of your purpose statement?
- Do your current women's ministry programs and activities reflect your purpose?
- If you have a purpose statement, has it been evaluated recently?
- Does your purpose statement adequately reflect the needs of the women in your church and community?

VISION

There is power in a vision that has been cast by the Holy Spirit into the heart of a leader. When looking over the purpose statement of your local church, does your heart begin to beat faster with passion for an area of ministry that lines up with the overall purpose? The passion of your heart is the beginning of vision. What makes your heartbeat quicken? What about a woman's life, world and relationship to Christ excites you?

Bill Hybels wrote the following about vision:

> Vision is at the very core of leadership. Take vision away from a leader and you cut out his or her heart. Vision is the fuel that leaders run on. It's the energy that creates action. It's the fire that ignites the passion of followers. It's the clear call that sustains focused effort year after year, decade after decade, as people offer consistent and sacrificial service to God."[6]

Vision really is where change begins. A clearly stated purpose gives you a foundation; for example, my purpose in life is to follow Christ. Vision, then, is the quickening of the heartbeat with the excitement of what it means to follow Christ and how that will change your life when it happens. What makes a vision so powerful is that it's not just a snapshot of a future hope; it's the energy and passion that stirs the heart to create that snapshot.

Three things happen when God imparts His vision into our hearts:

1. We recognize, or see, the vision.
2. We realize our hearts beat with the vision.
3. We responsibly take ownership of the vision and develop a plan of action.

Many times leaders recognize an area in life that they are so passionate about that they feel they were born for that very purpose! This is vision.

How does vision tie in to purpose? Once a purpose is clarified, it's time to define your vision. Vision is the desired outcome of the fulfilled purpose. For instance, if your purpose is "to help women grow in Christ," then your vision would state how that would happen: "The vision of women's ministry is to provide activities, small-group studies and special events that offer opportunities for genuine encounters with the true and living God." The vision may generate questions: *How does growing in Christ affect a woman's everyday life? What is the result of women growing in Christ? Where do we want these women to end up once they start growing?*

Now that the purpose is established and the vision is cast, it's time to take that next step, developing mission.

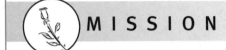

MISSION

Sometimes talking about vision, purpose and mission all in one breath seems confusing, doesn't it? How do they differ? Why do they all sound the same? Because of this confusion, many leaders give up and go forth without clear direction.

Mission is the feet that will be placed under the purpose and the vision. A mission is (1) an establishment of missionaries; (2) the work of spreading the Christian faith.[7] According to this definition, the mission is the work of the ministry. You can hammer out a purpose, be ignited with vision and cast that vision to your leaders; but without putting it into action, there will be no ministry!

How exciting to think of your women's ministry leadership team as a group of missionaries! You may not be in a third-world country, but you are in a country where women need a relationship with Christ. And sadly, many are not entering into this life-giving relationship—even within our churches. Christians sit week after week singing "Standing on the Promises," when they are just *sitting on the premises*! There is a mission field: a mission field for the lost in our communities, those who don't know Christ and those lost in self—who know Christ but are not following Him. There are women everywhere who need the Savior's touch. A women's ministry can change their lives through biblical instruction, fellowship and programs that meet their needs. Allow God to lead your ministry team in determining *purpose*, igniting them with *vision* and equipping them for the *mission*!

The next step is calling out the missionaries, defining the leadership structure for your women's ministry and igniting God's chosen team for effective leadership.

Notes

1. Bill Hybels, *Courageous Leadership* (Grand Rapids, MI: Zondervan Publishing House, 1995), p. 30.

2. Jill Briscoe, Laurie Katz McIntyre, and Beth Severson, *Designing Effective Women's Ministries* (Grand Rapids, MI: Zondervan Publishing House, 1995), p. 24.

3. Ibid.

4. "Who Is Cornerstone?" *Cornerstone Fellowship.* http://www.corner stoneweb.org/index.php?m=who+is+Cornerstone (accessed May 4, 2004).

5. "Women's Ministry," *Cornerstone Fellowship.* http://www.corner stoneweb.org/index.php?m=getting+connected&sub=ministries&mini stry=24 (accessed May 4, 2004).

6. Bill Hybels, *Courageous Leadership* (Grand Rapids, MI: Zondervan Publishing House, 1995) p. 30.

7. *Oxford American Dictionary*, s.v. "mission."

DEFINING THE
Leadership
STRUCTURE

There are different kinds of service, but the same Lord.

1 CORINTHIANS 12:5

Whether the women's ministry you are involved is in need of a face-lift or is in the planning stages, bringing definition to the leadership structure is an important foundational step.

Most women's ministries rest on a team of dedicated women who act as the ministry's steering committee. This steering team might be called the Women's Ministry Council, the Women's Ministry Board or the Women's Ministry Leadership Team. For the purpose of this chapter, let's refer to this group as "the council."

The size of the women's council depends on the size of the church, the number of women being served and the number of ministry areas being supported. In general, the most efficient size is between three and seven women, but the council could extend to 12 women in large churches. With the exception of church staff positions, each council member should agree to a specific term of service. The term of committed service should be about two years, which will allow women to serve on the council for a set period of time, establishing their gifts and making an eternal impact. A term agreement gives women the opportunity to rotate off the team without feeling like they're quitters. The final selection of who presides

on the council should always be made in agreement with the pastoral leadership of the church.

THE WOMEN'S MINISTRY COUNCIL

Diversity

Given the fact that God created us equal but different, it only makes sense that each woman on the council will be different in personality, gifting, experience and age. Difference is the spice that gives the women's team vision for different ministries. Though some women will have similar interests and needs, it is important for the ministry as a whole that the council be diverse, not a cookie-cutter representation of what is generally accepted within the church. It's important to resist the temptation to make friendship a determining factor in choosing a team. Yes, the team might get along better if everyone has similar interests or enjoys each other's company, but it can also easily become off balanced.

Consider the following story:

> Lee was the women's council coordinator at her local church. She loved people and wanted everyone to have a good time. She also had some very specific ways of looking at life and handling situations. Her way was nonnegotiable, as she really

believed her way was the *right* way. As the leader, Lee created an environment of fun and fellowship, as long as others did everything her way. Most women went along with Lee, as she was the voice of experience and a popular person.

But as the ministry grew, new women felt like outsiders because of Lee's unspoken rules for correct conduct within the group. The other women on the leadership team were all so much alike that any difference was not easily accepted. What started out as a ministry endeavor ended up as a social clique within the women's group. New women could not crack the exterior shell of the ministry team. Personal gifts and styles were not being utilized, and the ministry soon grew stale. They were a unit—as closely knit as any good dysfunctional family.

In order for balance to be restored, the entire ministry council needed a face-lift, and Lee could no longer be the only one with a voice. Through the guidance of a staff pastor, the women's council began to take a different shape. The women's council could no longer have the appearance or the activity of a well-established friendship circle. This was an important step in serving Christ within that local church. As a result, the ministry grew and women had a safe place to plug into. [1]

What can we learn from this?

- Resist choosing women with the same personality type or gifting.
- Resist choosing leaders only from a pool of established friends.
- Have a wide range of ages and experience on the council.
- Seek the Lord and godly counsel regarding council leadership selection.

Key Positions

Women's Ministry Council Coordinator

The selection of a women's ministry council coordinator will vary depending on the structure of the church and the preexisting ministry. The women's ministry council coordinator in a small church usually serves directly under the pastor or church-governing council (i.e., elder or deacon board). In a midsize to large church, she will most likely serve directly under a women's pastor or other church leader. In any case the women's ministry council coordinator should be organized, diplomatic and able to devote a sufficient amount of time to the ministry. The amount of time spent by the coordinator depends on the size of the church and the complexity of its ministries. In the larger church, this is quite often a staff position. Her spiritual gifts would probably include leadership and administration.

Council Administrative Anchor

As with most organizational structures, the council needs a secretary or administrative assistant to record minutes, keep the calendar and remind people of their responsibilities. She must be detail oriented, committed to attending meetings and efficient. She should also be a people person, dedicated to the ministry and skilled in computer use and e-mail correspondence. Her spiritual gifts would include service and administration.

Council Financial Coordinator

The council financial coordinator oversees all budgets and expenditures within the women's ministry. It is her responsibility to make sure each ministry provides a budget before any scheduled event. She will work closely with the women's ministry council coordinator, the church financial officer and the women who coordinate each individual ministry. In a small church, the job of council financial coordinator position could be combined with the council administrative anchor position.

Now you have a snapshot of the key ministry roles: the women's ministry council coordinator, the administrative anchor and the financial coordinator. In a small church, these three leadership roles may be the only members of a leadership team. In a large church, these key roles are the foundation that supports the rest of the ministry council positions.

Organizational Structure of the Ministry Council

In addition to the key roles, the women's ministry council could include an area coordinator and an assistant for each separate women's ministry within the church. Each ministry area should have a separate committee. The following list is provided to give you some ideas for organizing your own ministry areas. Small ministries would probably combine some of these areas. Large ministries might include more.

- **Spiritual Growth Coordinator** organizes Bible studies and other teaching ministries.
- **Encouragement Coordinator** organizes prayer chain, mentoring, visiting new members, etc.
- **Evangelism Coordinator** organizes events and activities with evangelistic emphasis.
- **Service Coordinator** organizes child care, service projects, hospital visits, etc.
- **Missions Coordinator** organizes information about missionaries and missions events.
- **Hospitality Coordinator** organizes greeters, decorations, refreshments, meals, etc.
- **Activities Coordinator** organizes crafts, social events and special groups.

Each area coordinator should be hand selected by the pastor or women's ministry council coordinator and asked to serve a minimum of two years.

The women's ministry council is made up of the council coordinator, the administrative anchor and the financial coordinator along with the area coordinators for each area of ministry that your group has developed. This council does not specifically plan events and activities; they serve primarily as the visionaries for the ministry.

Each area coordinator oversees the individual ministry to which God has called her, and her assistant and/or committee plans events and activities related to that particular ministry. Together with the women's council, each area coordinator helps maintain the integrity and mission of the women's ministry as a whole.

Some ministry leaders have likened the structure of a women's ministry to a tree. The image of a tree has the following advantages:

- It is alive.
- It has unlimited growth potential.
- It is designed to produce fruit.
- The branches are interdependent.
- It provides a place of refreshment.
- It grows upward, taking the major responsibility off the coordinator.
- It has a stable root system.
- It is extremely versatile.
- It allows for pruning without damaging the other branches.

In the tree model, the Bible, a board of elders, deacons, pastors or other governing group would serve as the roots. The trunk might represent the administration or the officers of your council. The branches would be the general areas of ministry. On the branches are the leaves, which might be the actual activities of the ministry (e.g., Bible studies, events, fellowship groups, service projects).

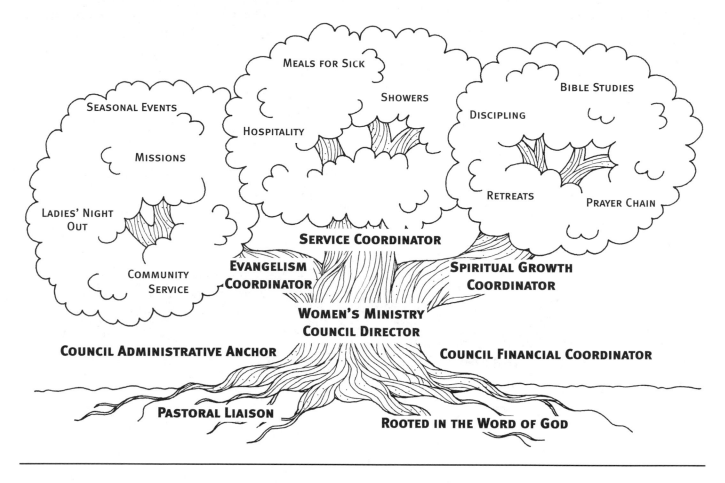

The tree illustration contains the following labels:

SEASONAL EVENTS

MISSIONS

LADIES' NIGHT OUT

COMMUNITY SERVICE

MEALS FOR SICK

SHOWERS

HOSPITALITY

SERVICE COORDINATOR

BIBLE STUDIES

DISCIPLING

RETREATS

PRAYER CHAIN

EVANGELISM COORDINATOR

SPIRITUAL GROWTH COORDINATOR

WOMEN'S MINISTRY COUNCIL DIRECTOR

COUNCIL ADMINISTRATIVE ANCHOR

COUNCIL FINANCIAL COORDINATOR

PASTORAL LIAISON

ROOTED IN THE WORD OF GOD

Women's Ministry Organizational Chart

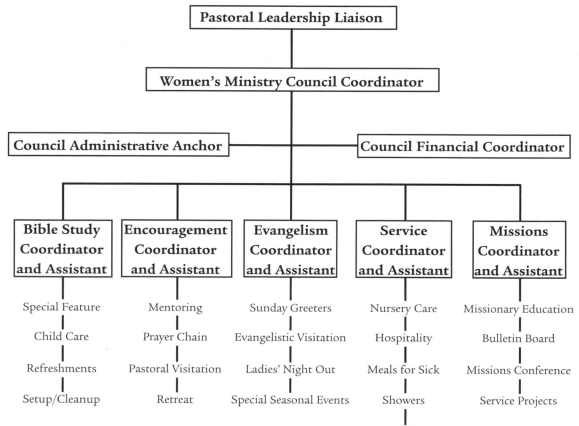

Pastoral Leadership Liaison

Women's Ministry Council Coordinator

Council Administrative Anchor

Council Financial Coordinator

Bible Study Coordinator and Assistant	Encouragement Coordinator and Assistant	Evangelism Coordinator and Assistant	Service Coordinator and Assistant	Missions Coordinator and Assistant
Special Feature	Mentoring	Sunday Greeters	Nursery Care	Missionary Education
Child Care	Prayer Chain	Evangelistic Visitation	Hospitality	Bulletin Board
Refreshments	Pastoral Visitation	Ladies' Night Out	Meals for Sick	Missions Conference
Setup/Cleanup	Retreat	Special Seasonal Events	Showers	Service Projects
			Decorations	

Council Meetings

When you start planning a women's ministry, the women's ministry council will want to meet frequently, even weekly at first. Once the council and the plans are established, monthly meetings should be sufficient. Plan meeting times and locations that are convenient for everyone involved. Depending on your group, you can conduct a businesslike meeting in a church conference room or a more comfortable meeting at someone's home that may include a meal.

Every meeting should include some growth material that will enhance the women as leaders. Have the council members review a leadership or other spiritual growth book together, practice Scripture memorization, do a devotional or Bible study, watch videos that are pertinent to spiritual growth or enlist a speaker who can provide leadership tips.

Part of every meeting should also include a relationship-building activity and a time for prayer.

The Meeting Agenda

Meetings without a plan or agenda can waste valuable time (see Sample Agenda on p. 47). It is the responsibility of the women's ministry council coordinator to set the tone of the meeting and keep it moving in the right direction (see the reproducible Sample Meeting Planner form on p. 48). The following list of productive meeting steps has been adapted from the *Women's Ministry Handbook.*[2]

1. Set the agenda before the meeting and send it to all council members before the meeting.
2. Clearly state the purpose of the meeting, and have the key agenda items written on a poster board, white board or chalkboard or overhead projector.
3. Prioritize the agenda into A-level items and B-level items. Place an A-1 beside the most important item, an A-2 beside the next, and so forth. All A items must be covered during the meeting. Place B-1 and so forth beside items that can wait until the next meeting if the meeting lasts too long.
4. Always deal with A items first. Juggle the agenda, but deal with the A-1 item while it's

fresh. Don't be diverted into believing the B-15 consideration will just take a minute.
5. Assign a time limit for discussing each item. This keeps members focused on important issues and helps discourage digressions.
6. Appoint a timekeeper. Make sure she has a watch and will bravely announce, "We've already spent 10 minutes on the potluck and we only posted 5 minutes for that subject. We need to move on to the next item."
7. Refer items that need further information or additional planning to a committee or an individual whenever possible. Assigning tasks to a committee or individual with plans to report back at the next meeting is sound management practice. It expands spiritual service, saves time and keeps meetings moving.
8. Cross off each item when completed.
9. Make allowances for uniqueness. For some members, making quick decisions can produce anxiety; they may need more time to process the information. For others, anxiety is created by the lack of decision. Keep the meeting moving by carefully managing the needs of both groups.
10. Understand your group's limitations. Only so much can be accomplished in any one meeting, so don't force every issue to a conclusion.
11. Reserve time at the end to recap the decisions and the assignments so that everyone is clear on what he or she needs to do.
12. End on time. At the end of the meeting, thank everyone for coming, remind them of the next meeting date and conclude with a time of prayer.

Building on Your Greatest Resource

The key is to build your ministry on the foundation that God has already provided for you—the women in your church and community. Ministry must be designed according to your own women's characteristics and needs. This will be different in each community.

It is important to remember that each church is different. In seeking to serve, the most important thing to do is seek the Lord's guidance when developing the groundwork for ministry.

In all your ways acknowledge him and he
will make your paths straight.

PROVERBS 3:6

LEADERSHIP QUALIFICATIONS

Being part of the council is a call and an appointment from the Lord that should be approached seriously. Though no woman is perfect, a woman serving on the council should be selected on the basis of her character, spiritual maturity, giftings and leadership ability.

When appointing women to the council, remain open to the leading of the Lord, remembering that nobody has it all together. Serving in this capacity will undoubtedly stretch each woman and produce spiritual growth. The most important aspect then is not perfection but calling and surrender.

Elmbrook Church in Wisconsin established qualifications for the coordinators serving on their women's ministry council. This qualification list could be applied to any women's council member, in any church.

1. She is a church member and regular attendee.
2. She models the following characteristics:
   - Obedience to God and His Word
   - Growing personal intimacy with God
   - Devotion to ministry
   - Humility
   - Integrity
   - Team spirit
   - Receptivity
   - Ability to delegate
   - Vision
   - Enthusiasm
   - Servanthood
3. She agrees to meet once every six weeks as a team with the women's pastor. (This has proven to be a tremendous time of laughter, camaraderie, spiritual growth, burden bearing and bridge building between each ministry branch.)
4. She mirrors Christ in her home and/or work arena.
5. She nurtures and develops the committee members in her charge by conducting a monthly committee meeting and staying in touch regularly. **Note:** Committee members are not required to be members of the church. Many women have joined a committee and then joined the church later or helped establish a vibrant ministry in another church.
6. She draws other women into leadership and encourages them.
7. She participates in a yearly team-building day.
8. Each year, she sets personal and ministry goals with the women's ministry council coordinator.
9. She maintains an advisory capacity upon stepping aside from the area coordinator position.[3]

Coordinator Assessment

During the summer months, each area coordinator should meet with the council coordinator to assess how she met her goals for the area of ministry that she leads. These coordinator assessment times can be excellent opportunities for friendship development, personal-needs analysis and encouragement as each area coordinator identifies ministry growth. It is also an opportunity for the women's ministry council coordinator to point out areas that need improvement. **Note:** The women's ministry council coordinator should go through the assessment process with a member of the pastoral staff or governing board of the church.

The following evaluation form is for coordinators to complete annually. This evaluation can be used when the women's ministry council coordinator or women's pastor meets with each individual area coordinator. The personal questions breed familiarity, relationship and friendship at spiritual and leadership levels.

Notes

1. This is a true story. Names have been changed to protect privacy.
2. Carol Porter and Mike Hamel, eds., *Women's Ministry Handbook*, (Colorado Springs, CO: Cook Communications Ministries, 1992), p. 69.
3. Jill Briscoe, Laura Katz McIntyre, and Beth Severson, *Designing Effective Women's Ministries*, (Grand Rapids, MI: Zondervan Publishing House, 1995), p. 98.

COORDINATOR EVALUATION

1. In review, what did your ministry look like this year?

   Highlights?

   Disappointments?

   Changes?

   Challenges?

2. Where would you like your ministry to be by the end of next year in terms of

   Equipping others

   Spiritual growth

   Leader recruitment

   Outreach

3. What are you planning to do to meet your objectives?

4. How will your progress be measured? To whom are you directly accountable?

5. How are the relationships within your committee?

6. What can the women's ministry council coordinator do to help you meet ministry goals?

7. What is your greatest personal need as one who serves in this church?

8. What is the one area of gifting to which you feel most called?

9. Are you operating in your area of gifting? Explain.

10. Where would you like to be in five years . . .

   Spiritually?

   Personally?

   Ministry-wise?

Women's Ministry Council Meeting

July 9, 10:00 A.M.

Opening Prayer

Spiritual Growth
Principles of leadership from the life of Deborah (Judges 4—5)

Friendship-Building
Pair up with another leader to share and pray about a personal need.

Branch Reports
Outreach Branch
 A-1 Evaluate the pool party
 A-2 Preview the Pumpkin Festival plans
 B-3 Update on missions

Spiritual Growth Branch
 A-1 Evaluation of summer Bible studies
 A-2 Preview of plans for fall studies and retreat
 B-1 Discussion of how to increase attendance at Saturday prayer meetings

Caring Branch
 A-1 Recruitment of new leader for Dial-a-Meal ministry
 B-2 Discussion of how to minister to new mothers

Service Branch
 A-1 Reorganization of coffee service
 B-3 Preview plans for Christmas craft day

Other Items of Business
Finalize plans for attending local seminar on biblical counseling

Prayer Time

Next Meeting
August 22—at Linda's house—bring a swimsuit and towel for the hot tub after the meeting.

Women's Ministry Council Meeting Planner

Date _____ Meeting Time _____

Location _____

	Whose Responsibility
Special Details (such as food served or someone's birthday)	
Opening Prayer	
Leadership Training/Devotional	
Friendship-Building Activity	
Agenda Items	

Next Meeting

chapter seven

Outlining
THE JOB DESCRIPTIONS

The body is a unit, though it is made up of many parts.

1 CORINTHIANS 12:12

Now that the council's purpose, vision and mission plan are in place, the coordinators who make up the team must have direction. Guidelines and clearly defined expectations are necessary to help people work to their potential. Within the boundaries of a clearly defined job description, make room for the flexibility of God's Spirit to move within the leadership and within each coordinator as each woman seeks to serve God in her position.

There are many benefits to a clear job description.

· It enables women to identify the ministry that is right for them.
· It helps to recruit the right volunteers.
· It provides a standard for service and performance, helping women understand the responsibilities of the position.

MINISTRY DESCRIPTIONS

The following pages are examples of job descriptions for various ministry areas. In a large church, more

area coordinators may be needed, and the ministry responsibilities might be spread out over many women. In a small church, there might only be a need for the three key coordinator positions (listed in chapter 6 on p. 39), plus a women's retreats and special events coordinator and a Bible study coordinator. These size differences would change the ministry descriptions. In either case, when God is working in the lives of His people, wonderful eternal things will happen—regardless of the size of the group. The key is to identify the jobs that need to be done and to do them with our whole hearts.

MINISTRY GROWTH

As you can see from the following pages, there is a variety of ministries that can spring from a healthy foundation in any women's ministry. As your ministry develops, you will need to make adjustments in the number of positions and the responsibilities of each position. As changes are made, be sure to outline the specific responsibilities and what is expected of each leader. This will help you avoid misunderstandings later.

It is suggested that a notebook for each ministry area be developed with the pertinent information for that ministry. Each area coordinator would add important information and tips as she carries out her responsibilities during her time of service. This notebook can then be handed off to the succeeding area coordinator. Having ministry notebooks is also helpful in case an area coordinator cannot complete her term or in the event of a sudden illness or family emergency.

The sky is the limit when planning and preparing for women. The key is seeking God and His will concerning the women you are serving. God will lead and direct each step taken when leading women into a deeper walk with Him. As time goes on and the needs of the women you serve are recognized, many ministries will blossom and grow—to the edification of the Church and the glory of God.

WOMEN'S MINISTRY COUNCIL COORDINATOR

Position

The women's ministry council coordinator sets the vision for and oversees the women's ministry in the church. As some say of this position, "The buck stops here."

Qualifications

- Public and private life above reproach
- Committed member of the church
- Consistent walk with Christ
- Prior experience in women's ministry at a leadership level

- Faithful, available and teachable
- Approved by the church governing council or board
- The blessing of her husband, if married
- Administrative skills
- A pastoral heart

Responsibilities

- Sets and maintains the vision for all women's ministries
- Oversees all of the women's ministries and activities
- Works closely with the church leadership while remaining teachable and accountable to a pastoral team member
- Leads the women's ministry council and council meetings
- Communicates regularly with women's ministry area coordinators and cares for them
- Provides leadership training and spiritual growth opportunities for the women's ministry council members

Organizational Relationships

- Responsible for overseeing administrative anchor and financial coordinator
- Responsible for overseeing women's ministry area coordinators
- Responsible to pastoral leadership of the church

Length of Ministry

- Being the coordinator is a key position, and a minimum two-year commitment is usually best for this ministry. If the women's ministry council coordinator is a paid-staff position, the term should remain open-ended. This term, however, can be terminated by the church's pastoral staff or a change of circumstances for the coordinator (such as family commitments or her husband's job transfer). If serving in this position for an extended length of time, the coordinator must learn to delegate, create teams and allow other women to serve in key leadership positions. She must always keep in mind that she will eventually train her replacement before retiring from this position.

WOMEN'S MINISTRY COUNCIL
ADMINISTRATIVE ANCHOR

Position

Women's ministry council administrative anchor assists and helps the council coordinator in all aspects of the operations of women's ministries.

Qualifications

- Public and private life above reproach
- Faithful, available and teachable
- Administrative experience
- Good relational skills and the ability to work with a wide variety of people

- Consistent walk with Christ
- Active member of the church
- Organized
- Dependable and flexible

Responsibilities

- Assists the council coordinator by fielding all appropriate calls and duties
- Mails and e-mails correspondence to women's ministry council members
- Mails and e-mails correspondence to church members
- Is active in all aspects of women's ministries and is available to assist when needed
- Chairs meetings if needed, as a backup to the council coordinator
- Schedules women's ministry events and coordinates events with church calendar
- Handles phone calls and appointment scheduling for council coordinator if necessary

Organizational Relationships

- Liaison between women in the church and the women's ministry council
- Responsible to the women's ministry council coordinator

Length of Ministry

- One year minimum service
- Council coordinator would appoint replacement when assistant resigns.

WOMEN'S MINISTRY COUNCIL FINANCIAL COORDINATOR

Position

The financial coordinator assists the women's ministry council coordinator by overseeing the budget of the women's ministries within the church.

Qualifications

- Public and private life above reproach
- Consistent walk with Christ
- Faithful, available and teachable
- Active member of the church
- Prior experience working with women's ministry council
- Administrative and accounting skills
- Dependable and detail-oriented

Responsibilities

- Coordinates women's ministry deposits with the church's financial officer
- Collects and records registrations from women for events and retreats
- Oversees the women's ministry budget and provides reports
- Advises the women's ministry council before it sets up budgets for special events

Organizational Relationships

- Responsible to the women's ministry council coordinator and the church financial officer

Length of Ministry

- Two years

BIBLE STUDY COORDINATOR

Position

The Bible study coordinator plans and implements the Bible study program for the women in the church.

Qualifications

- Public and private life above reproach
- Consistent walk with Christ
- Faithful, available and teachable
- Active member of the church
- Dependable
- Superior relationship skills; has a heart for women

Responsibilities

- Leads a team of women who are responsible for all aspects of planning and implementing women's Bible study: administration, hospitality, coordination of leaders and teachers, and worship
- Chooses curriculum with the input and approval of the church governing council and women's ministry council coordinator
- Coordinates the Bible study weekly and yearly schedules
- Schedules leaders training, including the hospitality and administration teams
- Is familiar with and stays within the ministry budget
- Stays on top of leader and program needs and advises the women's ministry council coordinator of pastoral needs that arise

Organizational Relationships

- Responsible to women's ministry council coordinator.

Length of Ministry

- This position can be rotated every two years, or it may be a paid-staff position in a large church.
- The Bible study coordinator is responsible for training her replacement.

RETREAT COORDINATOR

Position

The retreat coordinator organizes and oversees the planning of the women's ministry retreats.

Qualifications

- Public and private life above reproach
- Consistent walk with Christ
- Faithful, available and teachable
- Active member of the church
- Dependable
- Superior relationship skills; has a heart for women

Responsibilities

- Leads a team of women who are responsible for planning and implementing the women's retreat including registration, publicity, hospitality, program, event-site coordination, new-member coordination, skits, ice breakers and worship
- Plans and organizes retreat committee meetings
- Secures the retreat center a year in advance
- Selects speaker with committee input and the approval of women's ministry council coordinator
- Handles speaker's requirements
- Oversees all aspects of the retreat from the setup to cleanup

Organizational Relationships

- Responsible to women's ministry council coordinator

Length of Ministry

- Two years

MISSIONS COORDINATOR

Position

The missions coordinator educates women about how they can be involved in domestic or international missions and encourages them to become involved. The missions coordinator also creates women's teams for mission service projects.

Qualifications

- Public and private life above reproach
- Consistent walk with Christ
- Faithful, available and teachable
- Active member of the church
- Dependable
- Knowledge or heart for world missions

Responsibilities

- Researches service opportunities within the community and for the church-sponsored missionaries
- Organizes projects and teams in conjunction with the church missions committee
- Informs women about how they can help with these projects through volunteering time and/or materials and through prayer
- Responsible for women's missions committee members and project development

Organizational Relationships

- Responsible to women's ministry council coordinator and the missions' pastor or committee

Length of Ministry

- One to two years

DISCIPLESHIP COORDINATOR

Position

The discipleship coordinator plans and implements a discipleship program within the women's ministry.

Qualifications

· Public and private life above reproach
· Consistent walk with Christ
· Faithful, available and teachable
· Active member of the church
· Responsible about follow through
· Detail-oriented
· Superior relationship skills; has a heart for women

Responsibilities

· Chooses discipleship materials with the approval of the women's ministry council coordinator
· Develops a team of mentors
· Tracks progress of discipleship groups
· Pairs older woman with younger woman for discipleship
· Provides publicity and follow-up for the program

Organizational Relationships

· Responsible to discipleship program committee members and the women's ministry council coordinator

Length of Ministry

· At least two years of service

CAREGIVING COORDINATOR

Position

The caregiving coordinator connects women to one another for the purpose of meeting needs in times of illness, bereavement or other special circumstances.

Qualifications

- Public and private life above reproach
- Consistent walk with Christ
- Faithful, available and teachable
- Active member of the church
- Skilled in administration and people management
- Dependable and detail-oriented

Responsibilities

- Leads a team of women who provide meals, make hospital visits and personal care visits
- Provides training when necessary
- Organizes caregiving schedule
- Responsible for responding to the caregiving requests and assigning the women who have volunteered to work in the caregiving ministry

Organizational Relationships

- Responsible to the women's ministry council coordinator

Length of Ministry

- At least a full year of service
- Responsible for finding and training a replacement when term ends

BUILDING
THE *Ministry*

chapter eight

SURVEYING THE NEEDS OF
THE *Women*

This service that you perform is not only supplying the needs of God's people but is also overflowing in many expressions of thanks to God.

2 CORINTHIANS 9:12

Whenever your strategies are program focused rather than people focused, there will be little hope of really reaching the women you want to serve. Continually evaluating the purpose and effectiveness of the ministry and making changes where appropriate is important for the vitality of your ministry. Though change is usually met with resistance, your women's ministry council will discover that evaluation and the resulting changes keeps the ministry vibrant and alive with God's presence while meeting the true needs of the women to whom you minister.

It is common for a women's ministry council to base its ministry activities on a compilation of good ideas, but workable ideas alone will not be effective. You have to recognize the needs of the women to whom you want to minister. A Bible study for working women might sound like a good idea to a committee, but it probably won't work if the majority of the women in your ministry are stay-at-home moms.

People's needs should always be the first consideration when developing a program. After all, ministry is about the people, not the programs. The program is just a means to meet the needs of the people.

SURVEY THE WOMEN

After the initial planning of the women's ministry council, the next step for the council is to survey the women in the church. A survey will help in two ways.

1. It will identify the needs of the women.
2. It will identify those who can meet the needs.

No survey ever gets 100 percent return, but make it your goal to distribute the survey for the maximum return. Try handing out the survey at a church service or at the beginning of a women's event. Have the women complete the survey then and hand it in as they leave. If your church is small, you can conduct the survey by phone or in person.

It is important not to do a survey unless you are ready to act on the results. Too many times a committee loses credibility when surveys are handed out but the results are ignored.

On the survey, only ask the questions that will provide the information truly needed for the coming year. Surveying too far in advance makes the information useless when the time actually comes to start a ministry. People change and needs change, so make sure you stay current with the needs of the women in your church. An annual survey is a good rule of thumb.

An effective survey should tell you the following:

- The specific needs of the women you serve
- The ministries in which they are currently involved
- The ministries they are interested in adding
- The changes that need to be made to better meet their needs
- The characteristics of the women of your church as a group

It should also

- Be short and to the point.
- Include a place for the women to provide their name, phone number and e-mail and mailing address.
- List the current ministries with boxes to check if they wish to attend or help (e.g., Bible study, craft nights, women's dinners and teas).
- List specialized skills or interests needed in your ministries with boxes to check if they wish to help (e.g., meal preparation, word processing, decorating, speaking or teaching).
- Leave a place for the women to write in any special needs, interests or additional ideas for ministry that they might have.

Try to keep the survey to a single sheet of paper. The advantage of a survey is that it is easy to develop and review and it can be administered to a large group. The disadvantage is that a survey is only useful in obtaining very limited information.

It is difficult to communicate opinions beyond yes or no on paper. Surveys are often handed out at the end of an event when women are tired and want to leave, such as at the close of a retreat.

There is a sample of a women's ministry survey at the end of this chapter.

SURVEY THE LEADERS

If you want to keep the women's ministry current and relevant, truly meeting the needs of the women you want to reach, a "people study" is a good starting point. The women's ministry council should regularly ask and answer the following questions:

- Who are we trying to reach?
- Who is actually being reached?
- Which women in the church and community are we not reaching? Why?
- Has our audience changed? In what way?
- What are the greatest needs among the women in this community?
- What are our current barriers to ministry and how can they be removed?
- What are our ministry's greatest strengths and weaknesses?
- In what areas do we need to change?

This process should be done at least once a year, but it also might be a good idea to do it midway through a program year to make adjustments where necessary.

UNDERSTAND PERCEIVED AND ASSUMED NEEDS

Another way to gauge the success of the ministry is to define the perceived and assumed needs. A perceived need is one that people feel and recognize—such as their need for friendship, laughter and belonging. An assumed need may not be recognized, such as being accountable to others. Not all believers want that kind of openness and familiarity. However, as a leader you know that allowing God to break through the barriers that prevent familiarity will in turn meet an assumed need—the need for fellowship. As a leader you must be mindful of both the perceived and the assumed needs of the women.

Paying attention to several research methods—written surveys, phone surveys, expert opinion and focus group discussions—will also be helpful in establishing ministry analysis.

The expert opinion in the case of a church ministry is when an individual—such as a pastor, women's council coordinator or teaching leader—makes a decision on behalf of the entire group based on the individual's knowledge and experience. An example of this kind of decision would be selecting preaching topics or a teaching series or choosing a Bible study. The teaching leader, for instance, usually makes a decision based on what she knows about her group's needs. These kinds of decisions aren't usually subject to a vote.

The expert opinion method is best used for planning an overall program, setting goals and establishing overall direction for the women's ministry. It is not meant to be exclusive of the women's overall needs. The disadvantage to the expert opinion planning method is lack of ownership from the women themselves.

Special Instructions for Expert Opinion Makers

- Determine the needs of your target audience.
- Keep an eye on culture shifts (films, magazines, TV).
- Talk to other experts and leaders.
- Recognize that people vote with their presence— if you offer what people want, they will come.[1]

ORGANIZING FOCUS GROUPS

A focus group is another way to gather information. A focus group is a small group that is representative of the ministry audience as a whole. This small group should include 5 to 12 people who represent the various ages, life stages and needs of your ministry. A facilitator leads a discussion of relevant questions to discover the needs and interests of the women represented.

For a focus group to be effective, it must have a purpose and plan. The facilitator plays an important role. She will need to create an inviting atmosphere and encourage discussion. Serving a meal or light refreshments helps establish a relaxing atmosphere.

The Facilitator

- Welcomes the participants and makes them feel comfortable
- Leads the group in prayer
- States the purpose of the group
- Sets the tone
- Creates an atmosphere of acceptance, encouraging women to give honest answers and opinions

Someone else should record the women's comments so that the facilitator can focus on eliciting responses from the women.

Guidelines

1. Base questions on experience rather than theory.
2. Follow a list of predetermined questions, but be flexible as needed.
3. Start with general ideas and work toward specifics.
4. Do not allow women to move away from the topic at hand—control the discussion.
5. Avoid criticism of any kind toward any person or group.
6. Do not allow any one person to monopolize the discussion.
7. Record responses, when appropriate, on a flip chart, chalkboard or white board so that all can see. For example, you might write a list of Bible study topics or activity ideas for the group to rank in order of importance.
8. Make it fun to participate and an honor to be included.

Focus group discussions are especially helpful for a new ministry or for a church that is struggling with an existing ministry. Page 65 has sample questions for a focus group.

THE VALUE OF EVALUATION

Ongoing ministries will be more effective when they regularly evaluate their programs, making sure that they are meeting the needs and fulfilling their purpose, vision and mission. Evaluation should lead the ministry leadership to make changes where necessary and continue to do those things that are effective. Change can add spark and newness to any ministry if it is done for the right reasons. We must always remember that ministry is about people, not the programs. Determine the needs of the people first, and the program will follow.

Note

1. Jill Briscoe, Laurie Katz McIntyre, and Beth Severson, *Designing Effective Women's Ministries* (Grand Rapids, MI: Zondervan Publishing House, 1995), p. 28.

Annual Women's Ministry Survey

Please complete this survey and return it to the hostess table before you leave.

Name _____ Date _____

Address _____ E-Mail _____ Phone _____

1. Check the statement that applies to how often you attended women's ministry activities this year.

    ❏ Weekly   ❏ Once a month
    ❏ Only special events   ❏ This is my first time

2. Make a check mark beside the regular activities and special events you have attended this year.

    Regularly Scheduled Meetings   **Special Events and Activities**
    ❏ Weekly Bible study   ❏ Annual Retreat
    ❏ Monthly social   ❏ Fall Harvest Tea
    ❏ Fellowship group   ❏ Christmas Dinner
    ❏ Discipleship group   ❏ Mother-Daughter Tea
    ❏ Book club   ❏ Holiday Craft Night
    ❏ MOPS   ❏ Missions Fair
    ❏ First Place group

3. What is your favorite meeting, activity or special event? Please explain why?

4. What is missing from our women's ministry?

5. What new events, groups or activities would you like to see added next year?

Planning Events

1. What was your impression of this event last year?

2. What do you remember about the speaker's message?

3. What would you like to see repeated for this year?

4. What different type of event would you like to see?

5. In general, what have been the strengths and weaknesses of our women's ministry events this year?

6. What would make our women's ministry events better?

chapter nine

BEGINNING A
Bible Study
PROGRAM

Your word is a lamp to my feet and a light for my path.

PSALM 119:105

Every structure needs a foundation. Scripture tells us that the Word of God is to be our foundation and stabilizing force. Bible study should be the bedrock of any women's ministry.

> Everyone who hears these words of mine and puts them into practice is like a wise man who built his house on the rock (Matthew 7:24).

> How can a young man keep his way pure? By living according to your word (Psalm 119:9).

> For the word of God is living and active. Sharper than any double-edged sword, it penetrates even to dividing soul and spirit, joints and marrow; it judges the thoughts and attitudes of the heart (Hebrews 4:12).

> All Scripture is God-breathed and is useful for teaching, rebuking, correcting and training in righteousness, so that the man of God may be thoroughly equipped for every good work (2 Timothy 3:16).

These are just a few verses that point to the purpose of God's Word in our lives. We can find many reasons to begin a program to encourage Bible study in our women's ministry.

DESIGNING A BIBLE STUDY MINISTRY

Many Bible study programs are held in a home until growth necessitates a more structured program in a church. Some churches have informal gatherings in homes as well as an established weekly Bible study program meeting at the church. Both options will be explored here.

The Home Group

For small churches, a home Bible study group is a good way to begin a women's ministry Bible study program. A home group usually starts out as a potpourri of women who come together to study God's Word. The leadership of a home Bible study group may be informal, and it should include a hostess, a teaching leader and a coleader.

The Hostess

This woman is the person who opens her home and her heart, allowing other women to enter both each week. She has the gift of hospitality and a willingness to invite women into her home. If unable to host the Bible study in her own home, she may hostess at another woman's home (or even the church facility), using her gift of hospitality to see that the following are provided:

- Beverages and other refreshments
- Name tags
- Extra pencils or pens
- A smile and a greeting for each woman as she arrives

Although these items are the responsibility of the hostess, as the group grows, she may delegate various tasks to other women. Even in a small group, there can be a greeter and another woman who makes a snack schedule, calling to remind women when it is their turn to bring a snack to share with the group. It is important to remember that the primary role of the hostess is to make the women feel welcome, whether in her own home, in the home of another or at the church facility.

The Teaching Leader

This woman prepares the lesson each week and is responsible for leading the discussion. She must have the gift of teaching. In a small group, she will need to facilitate dialogue so that the teaching becomes more than just a lecture. She may plan time for teaching on that week's Scripture passage, followed by a time to discuss key points from the teaching. The teaching leader should not be the power figure in the group, but a fellow learner with the other group members. She is part of the Bible study committee, serving the women and making them feel safe and comfortable.

She is responsible, with the coleader, for choosing a book or curriculum to study. She should get approval from the women's ministry council coordinator, or the pastoral staff if there isn't a women's ministry council coordinator in the church.

Note: The Focus on the Family Women's Series includes Bible studies that are appropriate to use with women of all ages and walks of life. For more information, contact your local Christian supplier or Gospel Light at 1-800-4-GOSPEL or www.gospellight.com.

The Coleader

The coleader is prepared to fill in when the teaching leader cannot attend the group. In the meantime, she acts as the connecting arm of the group. It is her responsibility to make a group-contact list that includes home and e-mail addresses, phone numbers and birth dates. She is responsible for all necessary communication and also for letting the hostess know of any special dates for the upcoming week, such as birthdays. The coleader is also responsible for providing a study schedule to the group members and for ordering the books. She also collects the money from the women for any Bible study materials.

The coleader is to be a support for the teaching leader. She should be a part of the planning process and should help the teaching leader choose the appropriate study materials.

Note: When choosing a course of study, it's important to make sure the pastoral staff approves the study materials. And remember to consider the personalities of the women in the group. The study is to equip and enrich them, not to give a teaching leader a platform. For instance, if women are struggling because they don't understand what Christ did for them, a study in the book of Ephesians would be timely—not a study in the book of Revelation just because the teaching leader specializes in end-times teaching.

Sample Morning Schedule

8:45- 9:15 A.M.	Coffee and fellowship
9:15-9:25 A.M.	Prayer
9:25-10:00 A.M.	Teacher's presentation
10:00-10:30 A.M.	Discussion time
10:30-11:00 A.M.	Prayer
11:00 A.M.	Dismissal

It is good to have a general schedule outlined for the home groups, but keep in mind that the informality of meeting in a home requires some flexibility. However, you need to show respect to the women by beginning and ending the meeting on time.

In a home group, women may also be assigned prayer partners each week to help them connect with another woman throughout the week. A home group might also plan special gatherings such as a potluck dinner with spouses or significant others, or a night at the movies with the girls. The Focus on the Family Women's Series *Crafts and Activities for Women's Ministry* also has additional ideas for encouraging fellowship. Remember that a home group is more than study; it's a small community. It doesn't take much to start a group: attendance of five or six women is adequate to begin.

The Bible Study Program

In a mid- to large-sized church, the Bible study program is best held at the church. This creates a weekly gathering and meeting place for women, and usually provides onsite child care. Some women's Bible study programs choose an annual theme and study one course of material throughout the school calendar year. Others offer a fall class and a spring class, each with its own distinctiveness. Still others offer different electives based on a semester or quarterly schedule. All Bible study programs should plan for a Christmas break of two to four weeks from early to mid-December until after the new year. In addition, many groups do not meet on a regular basis during the summer months.

Each women's ministry council must decide what is right for the women to whom they minister and how God is leading them to meet the needs of those women.

Bible Study Leadership Structure

The following leadership structure will help you build a good foundation for an effective Bible study program:

- **Bible Study Coordinator** oversees the Bible study program with the support, advice and oversight of the women's ministry council coordinator. She is not a teaching leader (although she might lead a study group) but primarily a support leader that handles all the details and organization of the program. She directly oversees all areas of operation, including administration, worship, hospitality and leadership.

- **Administration Team Leader** organizes and plans how the team will accomplish its objectives. Her responsibilities include
  > Registering members
  > Making member rosters
  > Placing members in small discussion groups
  > Taking care of all correspondence
  > Handling of finances
  > Manning the welcome and information table on Bible study day

- **Worship Team Leader** organizes and plans the worship for the women's Bible study program. Though a team concept allows many women to use their gifts, one woman needs to lead and plan the worship experiences. The leader's goal is to create an atmosphere that allows women to leave the cares of the day behind, prepares their hearts to enter into God's presence and makes their hearts teachable.

- **Hospitality Team Leader** is responsible for the following:
  > Providing coffee and tea service on Bible study day
  > Decorating the coffee and tea area
  > Decorating the stage area
  > Monitoring and ordering supplies (e.g., napkins, cups, creamers)
  > Helping the leadership team with special events

The hospitality team arrives early and sets up and prepares the refreshments so that everything is ready when the women arrive. A beautiful, calming atmosphere will help draw the women in and make them comfortable.

- **Leadership Team Leader** oversees the needs of the small-group discussion leaders and the teaching leader(s). She works closely with the women's ministry council coordinator and the Bible study coordinator to provide the following:
  > Training leaders
  > Planning leadership meetings
  > Holding team-building events
  > Providing appreciation and encouragement to leaders
  > Communicating with the Bible study leaders by e-mail, phone and prayer chain

The number of women on the leadership team depends on the size of the church. For a Bible study of 50 women, there might be 5 small-group discussion leaders, 5 coleaders, a teaching leader and a assistant teaching leader—making the leadership team 12 women. In a very large church there could be 50 small-group discussion leaders, 50 coleaders and 5 teaching leaders—making the leadership team 105 women! Obviously the leadership team leader can't lead a team this size by herself; she will need help from the women's ministry council coordinator, who provides pastoral care, teaching and direction for the entire leadership team.

- **Prayer Team Leader** understands and believes in the power and importance of prayer. She gathers with the prayer team each week:
  > Before the study begins—a suggested 30 minutes prior to start time
  > During the summer while teams form and plans are made
  > To pray for the women on the member rosters
  > As special needs or circumstances arise

It's good to have a designated place for the prayer team to meet each week. The prayer team leader might begin with a passage of Scripture, after which the prayer team prays for that day's pro-gram, the small groups, the leaders, the teaching and other specific needs.

- **Child Care Team Leader** oversees the placement of child care workers, the purchase of children's curriculum and the use of appropriate meeting rooms. In some churches this leader might be a children's ministry staff person. In others, this person might be someone from the leadership team. In either case the goal is to provide excellent child care and teaching while the mothers are learning about God's Word.

Note: Gospel Light has many excellent age-appropriate resources for midweek children's programs. For more information, contact your local Christian supplier or Gospel Light at 1-800-4-GOSPEL or www.gospellight.com.

Keys to Effective Bible Study Programs

- Committed leadership
- Clear goals
- Warm, inviting atmosphere
- Organized structure
- Excellent child care or children's program
- Commitment to the study of God's Word

The Program Schedule

If you are planning a morning and an evening Bible study program, choose names for each group to give them an identity. One church calls their morning study Morning Break, and their night group Evening Edition.

Some churches offer an early-morning Bible study for working women who cannot come in the evening. This is usually attended by only a small number of women and can be held in a home, at a restaurant or at the church.

Sample Morning Study Schedule

8:45-9:15 A.M.	Fellowship and refreshment time
9:15-9:30 A.M.	Worship and announcements
9:30-10:00 A.M.	Bible teaching
10:00-10:10 A.M.	Move to small discussion groups throughout church facility
10:10-11:15 A.M.	Small-group discussion
11:30 A.M.	All children must be picked up by this time

Sample Evening Study Schedule

6:45-7:00 P.M.	Fellowship and refreshment time
7:00-7:15 P.M.	Worship and announcements
7:15-7:45 P.M.	Bible teaching
7:45-7:55 P.M.	Move to small discussion groups throughout church facility
7:55-9:00 P.M.	Small-group discussion
9:10 P.M.	All children must be picked up by this time

Sample Early Morning Study Schedule

6:00-6:15 A.M.	Fellowship and light breakfast (beverages and rolls or bagels)
6:15-7:00 A.M.	Bible teaching
7:00-7:30 A.M.	Group discussion

Some women's ministry Bible studies use a video curriculum for the main teaching session and then move into small groups for discussion. The following is a sample schedule for a video study format:

Sample Video Study Schedule

8:45-9:00 A.M.	Fellowship and refreshment time
9:00-9:15 A.M.	Worship and announcements
9:15-10:10 A.M.	Video teaching
10:10-10:20 A.M.	Move to small discussion groups throughout church facility
10:20-11:30 A.M.	Small-group discussion
11:40 A.M.	All children must be picked up by this time

The *Women's Ministry Handbook* describes the importance of Bible study:

A women's Bible study group can be many things. It can be a family where new believers can be born, where older sisters and spiritual mothers can nurture new believers and model for them what a growing Christian looks like. It can be a refuge for those who have been deeply hurt, a safe place to hear and learn new ways of responding to life.

To the woman in the marketplace the study provides a counterbalance to the dehumanizing work environment. To the woman at home with preschoolers, it provides adult contact and the stimulus to broaden her horizons. To the woman whose husband won't allow her to go to church on Sunday it provides a spiritual life line."[1]

Note

1. Carol Porter and Mike Hamel, eds., *Women's Ministry Handbook* (Colorado Springs, CO: Chariot Victor, 1992), p. 126.

SESSION EVALUATION

(For Leaders)

Leader _____ Coleader _____

Date _____ Attendance _____

Week _____ Topics _____

What were the most significant events in the meeting?

What weaknesses or problems did you see in the meeting?

What did you learn that you did not know before?

What follow-up is needed (e.g., a note of encouragement, a miss-you note, a phone call)?

STUDY EVALUATION

Leader _____ Coleader _____

Study Title _____

1. What was the biggest highlight of this study?

    What did you learn about yourself?

2. Has this study changed your relationship with God? If so, how?

3. Was there anything you didn't like about this study or the way in which it was presented? If so, please explain.

4. Our desire is to help women develop a deeper relationship with Christ and close relationships with one another. How might we improve in order to better achieve this goal in the future?

5. Additional comments or suggestions.

    Thank you for your honest evaluation of this study. May God continue to strengthen your relationship with Him and your friendships with other women.

chapter ten

Training
SMALL-GROUP LEADERS

Never be lacking in zeal, but keep your
spiritual fervor, serving the Lord.

ROMANS 12:11

Blessed are those whose strength is in you, who have
set their hearts on pilgrimage.

PSALM 84:5

❧

A pilgrimage is an extended journey with a purpose. Each of us as women are on a life adventure because our walk with Christ is an extended journey—a journey that has significance and purpose. When we seek to build a women's ministry, and particularly a Bible study program that leads women down a path of purpose, we need to choose leaders who are developed and trained.

CLEAR OBJECTIVES

After recruiting women for small-group leadership, the next step is to outline clear objectives for each leader. What is expected? How long will she serve? What are the practical applications of her ministry each week?

The small-group leader in a Bible study program is actually a facilitator of the study materials for that particular week. It's not her job to teach the material so much as it is her responsibility to help her group process the material.

Job Description

Small-group leaders commit to serving for the program year with a break at Christmas. Renewal of that commitment should be reviewed annually. Responsibilities include the following:

- Facilitating discussion of a group of 8 to 10 women in a small-group Bible study.
- Preparing for the study by doing the lesson each week, noting appropriate discussion questions.
- Leading in prayer.
- Regularly contacting group members, especially those who were absent or are in need.
- Contacting the coleader or another replacement if the leader can't attend.

It is important for the leader to view the women placed within her group as God-ordained. With this attitude, she will serve them as if serving the Lord. Her goal should be to help these women connect to God and to one another. As a leader, she should be available to point the women to resources available within the church that would pertain to the women's spiritual or emotional health.

Facilitation

Facilitate means "to make easy, to lessen the difficulty of."[1] The group leader should come prepared to break down the weekly lesson into manageable pieces so that the women can digest the lesson and apply it to their lives. The following are two processes that need to take place during the discussion

1. Digestion—This is when spiritual food or truth is absorbed into the women's hearts. The weekly meetings help to absorb the truth that has been studied during the week. A leader needs to ask herself, *What can I do as a leader to help the women absorb the truth in this lesson?*

2. Application—This is the experiential step in the learning process. The group leader challenges members to put the truth into practice and initiates discussion about how they plan to do it.

THE MEETING

Great meetings are a product of good planning and preparation.

Leader's Checklist

❑ I have completed the Bible study work necessary for the meeting.

❑ I have identified key points and prepared a meeting objective.

❑ I have developed a working agenda for the meeting time.

❑ I have prepared handouts or materials that the group will need.

❑ I have all the supplies needed for the group.

❑ I have contacted other members who will take part.

❑ I have confidence that I can lead the meeting with Christ working through me.

The Setting

If your group meets in a classroom, arrive early and set up a welcoming environment. Ideally, by the time the first group member enters the room everything is prepared—handouts are ready, chairs and tables are in place and all visual aids are in place.

If the meeting is held in a home, work with the hostess to provide an environment conducive to study and discussion. Distractions, such as family members, pets, radios or TVs, need to be removed from the area. Make sure there is comfortable seating for everyone.

The Extra Mile

The following are ideas to make the study even better:

- Themed table or room decorations such as pumpkins in the fall, Christmas decorations in December or hearts and flowers in February
- Candles
- Scripture cards for memorizing Scripture and Prayer Request Forms (see p. 81) for prayer requests
- Cake, other treats or a small gift when someone celebrates a birthday

Adding beautiful details tells the women that you care about them and that something good is going to happen during your time together. The leader need not take care of these details herself; she could appoint one or two group members to add the lovely details.

Facilitator Basics

- **Acknowledge everyone who speaks during a discussion.** "Mary, thank you. That was an interesting point." "Jessie, your thoughts on that verse add a lot to what we are talking about." Be sensitive to laughter and groans and remember that 90 percent of communication is nonverbal; watch for clues that the women are uncomfortable, embarrassed or getting bored.

- **Clarify what is being said.** Sometimes a person means something other than what she said. When you sense this is happening, look for ways to bring understanding and clarity, while remaining sensitive to the person involved. "Let me see if I understand what you are saying."

- **Generate discussion.** Don't try to be the answer person. Ask your group, "Let's open it up to the group. What do you think about what was just said?" Make sure not to dominate as a leader, just facilitate.
- **Summarize what has been said.** Offer statements like, "So far it seems that we have been saying . . . " or "Jill, could you try to summarize the key components of the discussion so far?"

The Right Kind of Questions

Opening Questions
These are often used as ice breakers, enabling women to get to know each other better. Relate the first couple of questions to the theme of the lesson, but make them light or even fun.

- Describe an incident in which you experienced [insert topic] during the last week.
- What do you picture in your mind when someone is called a good Samaritan?

Launching Questions
The following are questions that draw the group members into the study:

- What do you know about (or what do you feel about) [insert topic]?
- What do you think was going through Peter's mind at the time?
- What three commands do we find in this passage?
- How does this relate to you personally?

Guiding Questions
Even a well-prepared leader will need to spontaneously guide the discussion at times. Here are two techniques that can help guide a discussion:

1. *Rephrase the question*—Original question: What did Jesus mean when He said, "Now that I, your Lord and Teacher, have washed your feet, you also should wash one another's feet" (John 13:14)? Rephrased: What do you suppose it meant to wash another person's feet? How can we exemplify that action today?
2. *Personalize the question*—How would you respond to Jesus if He asked you that question?

Responding to Answers
Summarizing after a series of questions and answers allows the leader to acknowledge group members' contributions while maintaining biblical integrity and direction.

Remember to maintain good eye contact and a smile while speaking: "Thanks for sharing that" or "That's a great point." Or maybe "Okay, that is a response worth considering; does anyone else have a thought on that subject as well?"

Applying Lessons to Life
The goal of Bible study is not just information but transformation. These questions should encourage women to apply the lessons to their lives.

- What difference does this truth make to you?
- What changes will you make this week as a result of our lesson?

CURRICULUM TIPS

Published curriculum is a good way to involve a group in a topic without a lot of preparation on the leader's part. There are many offerings out there in the marketplace. Any study you use should be selected with care and used wisely. It should also be approved by the women's ministry council coordinator and the pastoral staff. The following guidelines will help you as you select and use curriculum:

- Curriculum should never drive a group. It is a mistake to forfeit opportunities for extended prayer or for caring for one another, never cut short a community-building activity because "we have to get through the curriculum." Jesus never said, "Go therefore into all the world and complete the curriculum." Your goal is to make disciples for Jesus who are obedient to Him, yielded to the Spirit and loving toward others.[2]
- Never substitute curriculum for teaching the Bible. Curriculum and study guides should be used to enhance the group's purpose and move people into the Scripture.
- Don't feel obligated to finish every question. Competent leaders know what questions to use and how many to use. Choose a few good ones. Often, two or three good questions followed by the right kind of discussion and Scripture reading is enough.

The Focus on the Family Women's Series offers women's studies that are appropriate for women of all ages and walks of life. For more information, contact your local Christian supplier or Gospel Light at 1-800-4-GOSPEL or visit www.gospellight.com.

PREPARATION

Focused preparation communicates care, sense of direction and leadership to the women in your small group. Carefully think through each lesson and determine your desired outcome.

- I want my group members to **KNOW**—learn the facts
- I want my group members to **FEEL**—embrace the truth
- I want my group members to **DO**—take action
- I want my group members to **PLAN**—obey God

See the Sample Meeting Preparation Checklist: P.L.A.N. for help in preparing for a training meeting.

POSTMEETING EVALUATION

After each session, take the time to ask yourself the following questions:

- What worked well?
- What did not work?
- What would I repeat?
- What would I change?

SAMPLE MEETING PREPARATION CHECKLIST

P.L.A.N.

P—Point

What will the meeting accomplish?
- ❑ Write out KNOW, FEEL, DO, PLAN statements
- ❑ Write out meeting agenda and meeting objectives

L—Logistics

Is the setting for the meeting prepared?
- ❑ Seating
- ❑ Table decoration
- ❑ Refreshments
- ❑ Background music or candles
- ❑ Visual aids and handouts
- ❑ Materials ready: pencils, pens, paper, extra Bibles, etc.

A—Activities

What will happen during the meeting?
- ❑ Ice-breaker activity
- ❑ Announcements
- ❑ Birthdays
- ❑ Group prayer
- ❑ Other:

N—Needs

What's happening in the lives of group members? Provide an opportunity to share needs and then pray.

Wednesday Night Bible Study Schedule

September

10	Leaders kickoff dessert at 7:00 P.M. Leadership ends 40 days of purpose, communion and prayer. Leadership anointed with oil.
17	Bible study kickoff and orientation
19	Leaders' night with special speaker: "Becoming a Leader with an Undivided Heart"
24	Bible study kickoff

October

1	Session 1
8	Session 2
15	Session 3
22	Session 4
29	Session 5

November

5	Session 6
12	Session 7
19	Session 8
26	Thanksgiving break

December

3	Christmas celebration and study review
10	Holiday break
17	Holiday break
24	Holiday break
31	Holiday break

January

7	Introduction to new study
14	Session 1
21	Session 2
28	Session 3

February

4	Session 4
11	Session 5
18	Session 6
25	Session 7

March

3	Session 8
10	Review
17	Closing celebration

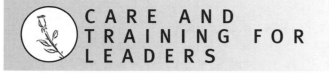

CARE AND TRAINING FOR LEADERS

Though leaders have needs as deep as other women, they often neglect having their own needs met while they are actively ministering to others. A busy ministry schedule piles up alongside family responsibilities and other obligations, leaving some leaders without the time to rest or refresh themselves.

As they spin in circles helping other people grow, they often end up tired, frustrated, empty or burned-out. Though it might not be noticed at first, the impact of a spiritually depleted leader is felt throughout the entire ministry.

The women's ministry coordinator has the responsibility to care for and help guard the leaders against burn-out. Leaders may individually benefit from

- Time off from ministry; a year's sabbatical from leadership responsibilities
- Leadership retreats for refreshment and new vision
- Theological training
- Specialized ministry training such as a counseling class or worship seminar
- A change of ministry opportunity
- Heart-to-heart relationship building with other leaders
- An occasional day of prayer and reflection away from all responsibilities

Women in leadership need to stretch and grow, but they may need reminders to take the time to do so. In building a strategy for leadership development, begin by identifying several key objectives that will be your program's foundation.

Here are five objectives for your consideration:

1. Involve your leaders
2. Inspire your leaders
3. Instruct your leaders
4. Instill passion and commitment in your leaders
5. Intercede for your leaders[3]

THE FOUNDATION OF BIBLICAL LEADERSHIP

Biblical leadership is the task of leading God's people into mutual ministry with one another for the purpose of building up the Body of Christ and reaching out to the world. In order to accomplish this purpose, leaders need to

- Establish a growing and maturing relationship with the Lord (see John 15:5)
- Sense a calling from the Lord to serve and lead people (see Exodus 3:1-10; John 21:15-17)
- Have a vision for building future leaders and developing the gifts of others (see 2 Timothy 2:2)

In Matthew 4:19, Jesus said, "Follow me," asking men and women to abandon their self-centered lifestyles to follow Him. In return, He gave them meaning and purpose. He nurtured, trained and equipped them for a mission that was far bigger than anything they could have imagined.[4]

Appropriate Motives for Leadership

To Glorify the Lord

"Whatever you do, work at it with all your heart, as working for the Lord, not for men, since you know that you will receive an inheritance from the Lord as a reward. It is the Lord Christ you are serving" (Colossians 3:23-24).

To Bear Eternal Fruit

"This is to my Father's glory, that you bear much fruit, showing yourselves to be my disciples" (John 15:8).

To Shepherd Others

"Keep watch over yourselves and all the flock of which the Holy Spirit has made you overseers. Be shepherds of the church of God, which he bought with his own blood" (Acts 20:28).

Leadership Requirements

- Maintaining a relationship with Jesus
- Following Jesus and His purpose
- Serving His people
- Leading His people in humility and love
- Obeying the Father in relationship with God and others

The spiritual leader will choose the hidden pathway of sacrificial service and the approval of His Lord rather than the flamboyant assignment and the adulation of the unspirited crowd. —Oswald Sanders[5]

Notes

1. *Oxford American Dictionary*, s.v. "facilitate."

2. Bill Donahue, *Leading Life-Changing Small Groups,* rev. ed. (Grand Rapids, MI: Zondervan Publishing House, 2002), p. 99.

3. Jill Briscoe, Laurie Katz McIntyre, and Beth Severson, *Designing Effective Women's Ministries* (Grand Rapids, MI: Zondervan Publishing House, 1995), p. 105.

4. Bill Donahue, *Leading Life-Changing Small Groups* (Grand Rapids, MI: Zondervan Publishing House, 2002), p. 37.

5. Oswald Sanders, *Spiritual Leadership* (1980), n.p., quoted in Carol Porter and Mike Hamel, *The Women's Ministry Handbook* (Colorado Springs, CO: Chariot Victor Books, 1992), n.p.

PRAYER REQUEST FORM

Name _____

Session Number _____

Phone _____

E-mail _____

Now it is required that those who have been given a trust must prove faithful.
1 CORINTHIANS 4:2

Prayer Request

**Remember:
Prayer requests
are confidential!**

PRAYER REQUEST FORM

Name _____

Session Number _____

Phone _____

E-mail _____

Now it is required that those who have been given a trust must prove faithful.
1 CORINTHIANS 4:2

Prayer Request

**Remember:
Prayer requests
are confidential!**

© 2004 Gospel Light. Permission to photocopy granted. *The Focus on the Family Women's Ministry Guide*

chapter eleven

DEVELOPING THE
Leadership
TEAM

*Recognizing who we are in Christ and aligning our
life with God's purpose for us gives a sense of destiny. . . .
It gives form and direction to our life.*

WORDS TO WARM THE HEART OF WOMEN

❧

Now that you have leaders, it is important to continue to develop them and take care of them. As you raise up leaders, keep these important concepts in mind.

- *Recruit*—Continue to add new leaders to the ranks and to increase your pool of potential leaders.
- *Regroup*—Form teams among your leaders and occasionally change teams to allow new relationships to form and a new gift mix to energize the ministry.
- *Respect*—Learn about varying leadership styles and the need to understand and celebrate differences.
- *Recognize*—Be generous to your leaders with hugs, encouraging notes, verbal praise, zany awards and other ways to say thanks.
- *Reflect*—Utilize focus groups, surveys and one-on-one reviews to facilitate more growth and mutual understanding of what is going well, what is lacking and

what could be improved. Always try to listen more than you speak during these times.[1]

Taking the time to train and care for the leaders will go a long way in building an effective women's ministry. This can be accomplished by providing training activities, leadership retreats and special events.

THE LEADERSHIP TEAM COORDINATOR

In most churches the women's ministry council coordinator would function as the leadership team coordinator, providing the training and care to the women she leads. However, in some ministries it might be wise to have another woman serve as the leadership team coordinator to ease some of the burden off the council coordinator's back. In that case, the leadership team coordinator would work side-by-side with the women's ministry council coordinator to provide activities and events especially for the leaders.

The leadership team coordinator might form an event team that will help with the planning, brainstorming, prayer support and footwork necessary for each leadership event. The women's ministry council coordinator and the pastoral staff should approve all leadership events.

LEADERSHIP RETREATS

A leadership retreat provides leaders with time and permission to relax. Along with some rest and relaxation there may be other objectives for the leaders on retreat, such as:

- Strengthening friendships
- Binding the leaders as a team
- Training and equipping
- Planning for the future
- Deepening personal devotional life

Planning a Leaders' Retreat

The leadership team coordinator should plan the leadership retreat in conjunction with the women's ministry council coordinator. The first step in planning a retreat is to find a place and reserve a date. Some possibilities for leadership retreat locations include the following:

- Hotels
- A bed and breakfast or a rentable house
- A park or forest preserve
- A local health club that has additional rooming facilities
- Condominiums or houses in a resort area
- Retreat center
- Vacation house
- The church facility (for a one-day retreat)

Determining the Goal

After determining the location and a date, the purpose or goal for the time together will need to be established. What do you want to accomplish? What do you want your leaders to experience or gain from this retreat? The following is a list of possible answers:

- Quiet time with God
- Reflection and evaluation time
- Relationship building
- Goal setting
- Vision casting
- Team building
- Fun

One way for the leadership team coordinator to determine the goal is by casually polling the leaders to get a pulse for what is most important for the group. This polling can be informal and conversational, rather than a rigid survey that might feel too structured or intrusive. Though it is serious business to determine a goal, you don't want leaders to feel like another number in the crowd. Rather, the idea is to allow them the space to state their needs or desires, giving you insight into what the majority of the women might need. This insight, along with prayer, can create an opening to hear from God concerning the needs of the leaders. Needs within a certain group can change and there should be no set formula for deciding the goal or purpose of the retreat.

Be cautious not to pack too much into one leadership retreat. A retreat that is too busy will defeat the purpose, allowing no one the time to rest or reflect!

After determining the goal, decide on a theme. A theme gives you a framework on which to build. Once the theme is decided on, every other aspect will more easily take shape. Find a key Bible verse that ties in with both the goal and the theme. The following sample plans should give you a better idea of how to prepare.

SAMPLE PLAN 1

Your Goal

Provide team building and an awareness of God's plan for women in relationship to others.

Theme

Living Love

Key Verse

"My command is this: Love each other as I have loved you" (John 15:12).

Activities

Invitation

The invitation would be in the shape of a heart with the verse on one side and the information on the other side.

Ice Breaker

Each woman will receive a special mug as she arrives at the retreat. Her mug will have another leader's name in it. This woman will be her prayer partner for the rest of the leadership retreat (or even the rest of the ministry year). The two will find each other and exchange information about each other using a sheet with questions. The last question should ask what the woman hopes to get out of the retreat. The prayer partners will join together for prayer after each teaching session during the retreat.

Craft Time

The craft will be making greeting cards. Enlist the help of the crafts coordinator to gather the materials needed for the activity. The cards should have an encouragement theme. The leaders could make several to use throughout the year to encourage their team members or the women they serve. Making the cards would signify the things we need to remember to do when in relationship with others.

Extras

A Scripture card, with a few selected verses from the weekend's teaching should be placed with a candy on each woman's pillow each night. If budget allows, each woman could be given a take-home gift, such as a leadership sweatshirt designed especially for leaders.

Here's another idea, from Elmbrook Church in Brookfield, Wisconsin:

SAMPLE PLAN 2

Your Goal

Equip, set goals and motivate leaders for a specific future ministry task.

Theme

Harvesting Eternal Fruit

Key Verse

"You did not choose me, but I chose you and appointed you to go and bear fruit—fruit that will last" (John 15:16).

Activities

Create name tags shaped like different fruits. A farmer gives a testimony about dependence on God when bringing forth a harvest.

Individual workshops might be entitled:

- Refreshing Rains of Rejoicing (praise and worship)
- Sowing Super Servants (how to lead others)
- Cultivating Caring Communication (relating in relationships)
- Yielding to Him (servanthood and selflessness)[2]

As you can see, there are certain aspects of a leadership retreat that are the same as any other women's retreat. The key when planning for leaders is to make sure the purpose is clear and the team-building intentional.

Just because women are leaders doesn't mean they can't have fun. Make sure to keep parts of any leader's event fun. Be creative!

LEADERSHIP SPECIAL EVENTS

Though a leadership annual or semiannual retreat is a good idea, it should not replace other events throughout the year. There are a variety of ways to keep the leadership connected on a regular basis.

You could hold quarterly meetings in which you provide a meal and child care. Have a clear goal in mind on what needs to be covered. Keep the leaders updated and trained. Provide a time for questions, answers and reflection. No decorations or fluff necessary; just provide:

- Food
- Child care
- Teaching materials
- Name tags

Some extra ideas, just for fellowship and connecting, include the following:

- Friendship tea
- Leadership breakfast
- Leaders' night out—see a movie or a play
- Leaders' sleepover—dinner, movies, manicures, pedicures, etc.

LEADERSHIP TRAINING

Most women who commit to leading feel the need for spiritual growth and equipping. Don't miss the opportunity to provide them with the means and the information to continue their spiritual journey.

Conferences and Seminars

Sending leaders to outside conferences or seminars is a good way to ensure their growth and focus on different aspects of ministry. Seminars don't need to have a leadership theme as long as they relate to the needs of the women attending. All women in leadership should keep themselves trained in areas that affect ministry. For instance, a seminar on women's intimate issues is not advertised as a leadership event. However, each of your leaders would grow tremendously by understanding more about an area with which many women struggle.

Ongoing Education

Many Bible colleges offer classes through the Internet or through video instruction. If you live near a Bible college, provide information for your leaders on the classes available.

Classes

There are many special classes that relate to specific life situations. These are good for your leaders to attend. For instance, a Mothers of Preschoolers (MOPS) leader should be encouraged to attend classes that relate to early motherhood, parenting or other classes offered by the MOPS organization. A first-aid class offered by the Red Cross or a class on group dynamics might also be helpful.

Leader Bible Studies

Provide Bible studies specifically for leaders. Even though the women are leaders, never assume that they know all the basics. And even if they do, everyone needs constant refreshing.

Books and Resources

A list of books and resources that are relevant to where your leaders are in their life stages can be a huge asset to the leader who desires deeper growth. Consider having the leaders all read and discuss a book that is pertinent to leadership or other aspects of spiritual growth. The appendix at the back of this book contains a wealth of information.

CARING FOR YOUR LEADERS

It is often the leadership in the church that can get overlooked in time of need. Make sure that you connect with the women in your leadership, and that you have pertinent information about them. Have your leaders fill out an information sheet to keep the information close at hand. The following list includes some of the information you might want to gather:

- E-mail address, home address and telephone number(s)
- Occupation
- Husband's name (if applicable)
- Names and ages of children (if applicable)
- If she homeschools her children
- Birth date
- Favorites hobbies, colors, music, etc.

With this information, you can begin a leaders' e-mail loop, a leaders' prayer chain and a leaders' birthday file. All of this adds up to more connection, team building and care. Also the leader who is cared for learns by example how to care for others.

Leaders in Need

If the church is small, it is easy to stay in touch with each leader's needs. If the church is large, a point person may have to be chosen to make the women's ministry council coordinator aware of a leader's need for pastoral care. This care might come in the form of a card, a call or a meal.

If you are a leader, remember you are part of a team. Team = Together Everyone Achieves More!

Notes

1. Jill Briscoe, Beth Severson, and Laurie Katz McIntyre, *Designing Effective Women's Ministries* (Grand Rapids, MI: Zondervan Publishing House, 1995), p. 121.
2. Ibid., p. 126.

LEADERSHIP INFORMATION SHEET

Name _____

Ministry involvement _____

Occupation _____

Address _____

Home _____ Phone _____ Cell _____

Work _____

E-mail _____

Birth date _____ Husband's name _____

Children's names and ages (include grandchildren if you have them) _____

_____

_____

Favorite color _____

Favorite activity _____

Favorite food _____

Favorite place _____

Hobbies or things you like to do _____

Favorite author _____

Favorite movie _____

Where are you at in this season of your life?

_____

_____

_____

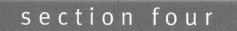

EXPANDING THE *Ministry*

chapter twelve

TAKING CARE OF THE
Children

Whoever welcomes one of these little children
in my name welcomes me.

MARK 9:37

Wherever women gather the need for child care exists; child care is a program that is a vital ministry all by itself. Every church handles child care differently. For some churches, the children's ministry department handles all child care. In some, it is the responsibility of each ministry to provide its own child care. In either case, the children are important and reliable care of children must be a consideration in any good women's ministry program.

THE PURPOSE OF CHILD CARE

The threefold purpose for the child-care arm of any women's ministry is to provide support, safety and nurturing.

Support

Child care exists to support the women who attend women's ministry functions. The simple fact is that many mothers would not be able to participate in these activities if child care were not available. The women will enjoy their ministry experience so much more when they feel secure in leaving their children in the hands of competent, loving child-care workers. This is especially important in outreach events for which the main purpose is to draw women from the community.

Safety

The safety of a child should never be compromised. The child-care coordinator should develop child-to-adult ratio guidelines, bathroom policies and behavior policies that will ensure the safety of each child. The helpers will need to be screened and trained.

Nurture

The main purpose for a child-care ministry should be that every child feels loved by God and by His people. The mothers will also feel loved when their children are nurtured by caring workers. It is also important to provide age-appropriate teaching for children over one year of age. This can be accomplished through the use of published curricula such as *Little Blessings* and *KidsTime* programs (available from Gospel Light),[1] or by developing your own materials.

Paid or Volunteer

Many churches use volunteer helpers for small groups needing child care, but when there are many children, better care can be provided by hiring and training child-care workers. Another option is to have one or two paid workers with a team of rotating volunteers to assist them. It is very important to have at least one team member who is a consistent presence in the care center so that there is someone to guard the standards and who knows the needs of the children who attend. It is also important that the children have a few familiar faces to make them feel more comfortable.

Payment could be taken care of through women's ministry offerings or through charging each woman a small amount per child in the child-care program. Many women's ministries take a monthly offering that is just for child care. The women with grown children (or no children) can give toward child care to ensure that the younger women have peace of mind during Bible study. Paid child-care workers should be given fair compensation for their time; pay should be based on local averages and state regulations. The amounts should be made clear to all parties at the time of program registration.

Child care can be charged by semester or paid for weekly when the child is dropped off. It might be helpful to sell child-care coupons to the women at the beginning of a ministry season. A coupon would then be placed in a basket when checking in the child for that day. In the case of a one-time event, women can pay the arranged amount per child for that event only.

FINDING CHILD-CARE WORKERS

There are usually women willing to volunteer to help with the children for a one-time event. But when the meetings are each week, it is often harder to find volunteers that will be consistent and reliable. One way to do this is to develop a child-care team that rotates so that each group of women would work once a month. Another way to provide consistent child care is to hire child-care workers for regularly scheduled weekly meetings.

Many churches may already hire one or more child-care workers for Sunday services who can also serve during the week. This is the ideal arrangement. If your church does not have such a person on staff, you might call other churches in the area who might

be willing to share their paid staff during the week.

The following are additional possibilities for paid child-care workers:

· Homeschooled teens (with adult supervision)
· Retirees
· College-aged women with flexible schedules

Conduct

All paid child-care helpers are to conduct themselves in a professional and Christlike manner. Care and attention should be given completely to the children in the room. Homework, cell phones and video games are examples of distractions that must be discouraged. Child-care workers should provide age-appropriate Bible lessons, crafts, activities and group games to the children under their care.

Wages

Wages should be proportionate to the minimum wage scale in your state. The following is an example from one California church that pays child-care workers for a large weekly women's ministry:

· Junior-high age helpers—$5.00 per hour
· High school workers—$7.50 per hour
· Adult caregivers—$8.50 per hour

This same church pays by check directly through the church accounting department. All child-care employees are required to fill out appropriate IRS forms.

Note: When paying workers under 18, check with your state's labor laws to make sure you comply with all legal requirements.

Check-In/Checkout
· All workers should clock in at least 15 minutes before a shift begins, and clock out once all children have been picked up and cleanup is complete.
· Provide a check-in/checkout sheet for the mothers to complete when they drop the children off. If there is more than one activity going on during the meeting time (i.e., several small Bible study groups

meeting at the same time), be sure to have mothers write down where they will be.

Cleanup

In general, the facility should be left in better condition than it was found. All bowls, pitchers and snack items should be cleaned, sealed and put away. Also, all tables, chairs, stickers and sheets should be returned to the appropriate location. One woman should be designated to make sure everything is clean and that all linens used will be washed and returned promptly. The following are some additional tasks:

- Toys should be sprayed with cleaner and wiped dry with paper towels or cloth towels after which toys need to air dry for 10 minutes.
- Empty all trash cans; replace trash can liners.
- Vacuum the carpets, especially if crumbs from the snack or mess from a craft is on the floor.
- Bring all lost and found items to a designated area.

CHILD-CARE WORKER/CHILD RATIO GUIDELINE

Each church should develop ratios based on the size of the room and facility the children are in. The following ratios are a general guideline.

Nursery—0 to 23 months

- Nursery: One worker for every two babies—maximum of 10 babies in the room.
- Toddlers: One worker for every five toddlers—maximum of 15 toddlers in the room.

Two- and Three-Year-Olds

- Two-year-olds: One worker for every six two-year-olds—maximum of 18 two-year-olds in the room.
- Three-year-olds: One worker for every seven three-

year-olds—maximum of 21 three-year-olds in the room.

Four- and Five-Year-Olds

- Four-year-olds: One worker for every eight children—maximum of 16 children in the room.
- Five-year-olds: One worker for every eight children—maximum of 24 children in the room.

ILLNESSES

It is a good idea to post the following standards prominently by the entrance:

- Children known to have symptoms of fever, diarrhea, vomiting, cold or flu should not be in class.
- Children known to have chickenpox, measles, pinkeye, lice or other contagious illness should not be in class.
- Child-care workers should not come to work if they are ill.

It is tough to turn away a child whose mother may be at her wit's end with a sick child and needs the respite that the women's ministry can provide. However, most mothers realize the importance of not infecting a whole nursery full of children.

CHILD-CARE WORKERS' RESPONSIBILITIES

Like all ministries, the child-care workers should have very detailed descriptions of what is expected of them. The following is an example of standards:

- Arrive 15 minutes before your scheduled shift.
- Never leave children with anyone under the age of 16. If you need to leave the class area, always notify the child-care coordinator or other adult child-care worker.
- Place all of one child's belongings in the

appropriate storage spot.

- Be sure each child has a name tag and a claim tag. (A claim tag with the child's name and parent's name should be given to each mother for each child she leaves. No child should be released to anyone who does not have a claim tag.)
- Collect claim tag (and nursery call pager, if your church has a pager system) from each mother when child is picked up.
- Check diapers frequently. Follow proper hygiene guidelines when changing diapers. (These guidelines should be posted in a prominent place near the changing table.)
- Diaper changes should be done in the presence of another adult.
- Wear your ID nametag!
- Dress comfortably and appropriately for the age of your class.
- Scan room for dangerous items and broken toys, and remove.

The child-care coordinator is responsible for making sure all child-care supplies are replenished after each event.

MINISTRY TO THE CHILDREN

There are many age-appropriate curricula materials that can be used for the children's portion of the women's ministry.[2] The child-care coordinator should arrange for materials or craft supplies to be available. Any time children can be taught truth, the opportunity should be taken. Instead of treating child care like another logistical hassle, ministry to the children should be viewed and planned with as much vision as the rest of the women's program.

Notes

1. Gospel Light has produced age-appropriate materials: The *Little Blessings* program (for infants and toddlers and *Little KidsTime* for ages 2-5). For more information, contact your local Christian supplier or Gospel Light at 1-800-4-GOSPEL or www.gospellight.com.
2. Additional resources are listed in the appendix at the end of the book.

chapter thirteen

Reaching Women
WHERE THEY ARE

Therefore, as we have opportunity, let us do good to all people.

GALATIANS 6:10

❧

Always keep in mind that ministry is about the people and not the program. We need to always be working toward meeting the needs of the women that God has led to our ministry. Women wear many hats, go through several life stages and have a variety of needs. The importance of providing a ministry that meets these needs cannot be underestimated. Chapter 8 discussed how to survey the needs of the women in your church. The information from those surveys will make it easier to meet the needs of the women in your ministry.

There are a variety of ministries that meet women's needs across the board. A weekly Bible study would be a perfect example of a ministry that meets the needs of a large target audience; a women's retreat is another example. Within the context of each ministry, defining a clear direction requires spiritual discernment and practical application survey results.

The following are a few questions the leadership team might ask:

· What is the greatest personal need right now in the lives of the women we serve?
· What ministry is well attended and seems to work?

· What new components and/or events do we need to meet the needs of the women in our church?
· What is the primary demographic this ministry reaches? Single? Married? College students? Career oriented? Mothers? Grandmothers? Empty nest? Divorced? Single parent?
· What group or situation seems to need the most immediate attention?

In surveying women's needs in one local church, the theme of depression, disappointment and low self-worth kept rising to the surface. It became obvious that women struggled with these life and identity issues and lacked a biblical perspective on their value as God's women. The next obstacle women faced was maintaining their marriage relationships. This was followed closely by lack of personal friendships. Add in exhaustion from child caregiving in the early parenting years and you have a snapshot of needs. The need list looked like this:

· Low self-worth, depression
· Marriage relationships
· Lack of friendships
· Motherhood stress

This local church's next tasks were to analyze their present program and decide how to add elements that would address these needs.

BUILDING YOUR MINISTRY

Once the church discovered where the women were in their life circumstances, the challenge for the leadership team was to create or build new ministries to meet these specific needs. Let's look at how this particular church leadership handled this challenge.

Women's Bible Study

The women's ministry council chose a topic that would help women in the areas the survey revealed. They chose *Breaking Free* by Beth Moore for their Bible study. In the context of the Bible study program, the women met weekly in small groups in which they connected with God and each other, addressing their need for female friendships. These small groups kept the same members for the entire Bible study session. The group leader planned offsite activities in which the women could further develop their friendships. Onsite child care was provided each week for two hours, providing a break time for the mothers of small children who might feel overwhelmed. These three areas of refreshment cannot heal a marital conflict, but they can certainly help renew a wife, which can have positive effects on her relationship with her husband. The development of friendships and the topic of the Bible study helped the women deal with their feelings of low self-worth and depression. This Bible study program sought to address all four felt needs found on the survey.

Special Classes or Seminars

Each year this particular women's ministry plans a special seminar day. This year, given the results of the survey, the women's ministry council decided to create a special class dedicated to strengthening marriage relationships. "The Excellent Wife" was the theme. A speaker led the key teaching while local women provided mentoring and workshop teachings that complemented the theme. After the seminar, they formed a new study group, and many women began a 12-week study that took them on the journey of being a more excellent wife. This helped meet the needs of the married women who were struggling in their marriages.

Friendship Tea

Each spring this church hosted a special event designed to meet the needs of the women in the church. To meet the need for more friendships, the women's leadership decided to host a friendship tea which could help develop the women's friendships. They planned the tea for a day in the month after the Bible study ended. After the friendship tea, a new group was formed to launch a study using Dee Brestin's *The Friendship of Women*. This was a lighter study that would bring women through the summer months.

Ladies' Night Out

While planning special events, the leadership chose to dedicate one of their quarterly ladies' nights out to mothers of all ages. They brought in the Mommies, a guest comedy troupe, and the act was hilarious. Women laughed at the calamities faced every day by mothers everywhere; they wept tears of joy over what children can bring to life and left with courage to carry on.

EXPANDING YOUR WOMEN'S MINISTRY

The women's ministry council coordinator, along with the women's council, should plan a vision day. That day should be a time to brainstorm and cast new vision based on the needs represented in the survey. From the brainstorming session you will get a list of ideas and themes to take to prayer.

The day's schedule might look like the following:

Vision Day Agenda

8:30-9:30 A.M.	Continental breakfast and fellowship
9:30-10:15 A.M.	Survey results presented
10:15-10:30 A.M.	Break
10:30-11:30 A.M.	Brainstorming session
11:30 A.M.-12:30 P.M.	Lunch
12:30-1:00 P.M.	Prayer and worship

| 1:00-3:00 P.M. | Evaluation and planning of calendar year |
| 3:00-3:30 P.M. | Assignments given to ministries |

Before the council starts brainstorming, make sure you have a firm understanding of the brainstorming concept. Brainstorming is a simple technique that can generate numerous ideas or solutions to a problem by suspending criticism and evaluation until another time during which the suggestions will be evaluated.[1] In the case of the sample schedule, the evaluation and selection of the activities were done on the same day, but in some cases they might be done at a separate meeting.

A large white board, chalkboard or large pad of paper should be available. The following guidelines are suggested for the brainstorming session:

1. Record all ideas.
2. Do not comment on anyone's ideas.
3. Do not make judgments.
4. Accept repeated ideas.

After an intense bout of brainstorming, it is suggested that the group take a break, either for a snack, meal or a walk to process the ideas. When the women return, the ideas can be evaluated, and the team can work on establishing a clear vision for all areas of the women's ministry. It is suggested that you cover the following:

- Decide on the purpose for the year.
- Develop a program for the season.
- Determine the calendar of women's events for the program year.
- Delegate responsibilities to the appropriate ministry coordinators.

As the leadership team surveys the calendar year, dates can be assigned based on each ministry's needs. Each ministry committee should make the detailed plans for the actual events at a later date.

The following events are listed to help you consider different ways to minister to specific needs. Each of these events can be adapted for any size church.

Ladies' Night Out

Plan a quarterly evening out just for the ladies. This might be held at the church with guest musicians or speakers and dessert. In a small church, this event could be held at a restaurant banquet room or in a large home. Although primarily meant for the women in the church, it could also be a good form of outreach.

Women's Retreat

An annual retreat weekend can be held the same weekend each year so that the women can plan ahead. The retreat is usually held at a hotel or retreat center but can take place in rented condos or a large vacation cabin for a smaller group.

Christmas Event

Hold an annual brunch, dinner or tea to usher in the Christmas season. Provide special music, décor and speaker. This is an excellent opportunity for an outreach event.

Spring Tea

Hold an annual tea in a nice garden, tea room or at your local church. Some groups do this each year around Mother's Day. Another option might be to hold one in the fall to introduce the plan for the year.

Mothers of Preschoolers (MOPS)

MOPS is a national organization that seeks to meet the needs of young mothers and their children. This is a great ministry for your church to provide for your community. MOPS meets twice a month throughout the school year and is specifically designed to reach out to the unchurched.

Craft Nights

Craft nights are great for those women who desire to express themselves creatively. This evening could be held a two or three times a year and should be a time for fellowship and fun. The women can make a predetermined craft as instructed by the craft leader or they could bring a specific craft that they are working on such as needlework. This can be a wonderful opportunity to invite women from outside the church.

Another idea is to incorporate a simple craft at the group's monthly (or even weekly) meeting. See the Focus on the Family *Crafts and Activities for Women's Ministry* (Gospel Light) for additional ideas.

Book Clubs

This group reads a specific book during the month and then gets together to discuss it. A book club can be held in homes, coffee houses or at your church. Beverages and light refreshments should be made available.

Heart Groups

For women who cannot commit to weekly study, the heart group is a monthly fellowship option that enables women to be connected to a smaller group of women. A group of 8 to 10 women meets once a month in a home and are led by the heart-group hostess. The group's goal is provide an opportunity for women to encourage each other, pray and share. Each month there is a theme and a selected Scripture passage that the group discusses.

Heart-to-Heart Care

Need someone to talk to? Heart-to-heart pairs women who can help carry the other's load. There's nothing like walking through your grief experience with another who has been there before you. This ministry is brought together on an as-needed basis.

Fitness and Weight Loss

Our bodies are the temple of the Holy Spirit. Women who struggle with weight-related issues often welcome a fitness ministry within a church. First Place is a national organization that has a wide array of materials for starting such a group within your church.[2]

Unequally Yoked

Women whose husbands don't share their faith face some very specific challenges. In one church this group is called "Pillars of Faith." These women seek to strengthen one another in the Lord, despite their unequally yoked marriages. Groups might meet twice a month for support.

Heart 'n' Home Mentoring

Young women today are often not familiar with the world of homemaking or child rearing. In this particular ministry, young women are paired with a heart mom and a home mom for six-week sessions. The heart mom helps the young women concentrate on issues of the heart while the home mom mentors in household areas. The six-week sessions usually consist of eight women and two mentors who meet together once a week in a home setting.

Your women's ministry might want to develop other forms of mentoring. For more information about mentoring programs, see p. 144.

Discipleship Groups

Operation Timothy has long been a favorite in discipleship programs. This is where a Paul (a more spiritually mature believer) takes a Timothy (a new believer) through the basic foundations of the faith. One course that gives new believers a solid foundation is *Beta* (from Neil Anderson and Gospel Light).[3] These discipleship commitments should last at least 12 weeks, but they might last as long as one year.

Women in the Workplace

More and more churches are forming groups specifically for women who have entered the corporate world. These groups usually meet once a month for a business and inspirational breakfast, brunch or luncheon.

Prayer

Prayer groups should be an integral part of every women's ministry. Moms in Touch is a national organization that encourages women to meet together to pray for children in a specific school or school district. Prayer groups, for any purpose, can be held weekly or monthly. Prayer group meeting frequency is often dependent on the level of need and/or interest of the women in the ministry. Developing a group of prayer warriors to uphold the women's ministry in your church will reap a rich harvest.

Notes

1. Jill Briscoe, Laurie Katz McIntyre, and Beth Severson, *Designing Effective Women's Ministries* (Grand Rapids, MI: Zondervan Publishing House, 1995), p. 40.
2. For more information on the First Place program, see the appendix.
3. For more information on Beta, contact your Christian supplier, or contact Gospel Light at 1-800-4-GOSPEL or www.gospellight.com.

chapter fourteen

Reaching Women
THROUGH RETREATS

Come, let us sing for joy to the LORD; let us shout aloud to the Rock of our salvation. Let us come before him with thanksgiving and extol him with music and song.

PSALM 95:1-2

Now is the time to give your ideas legs. Your women's ministry council has spent time and energy pouring over the surveys and women's needs; they have discussed the best ways to reach into the women's lives. Now it's time to prayerfully plan. The next couple of chapters outline in depth how leaders can plan and prepare for retreats and special events.

Try not to get caught up in looking for program perfection, instead take the time to pray for people who need life change. It's time to watch God work by making resources available so women can come to a place where they can connect with Christ and other women.

PLANNING THE RETREAT

Why Have a Women's Retreat?

- To relieve women of the routine and pressures of daily life so they can focus wholly on seeking God
- To strengthen women spiritually through concentrated teaching

- To provide uninterrupted fellowship time with other Christians
- To provide an environment for unbelievers to see Christ in the lives of believers[1]

Retreat Leadership

If this is your church's first women's retreat, pray for a group of women who share your vision. Meet to pray and to plan. Be willing to start small. You can either combine your retreat with another church, or plan one just for the women in your church. Some denominations have a denominational retreat. Combining your retreat with others will allow you to draw on the resources of a wider group of women and possibly bring in a more seasoned speaker, worship leader and program. However, a small retreat can present more opportunities for bonding.

The first action in planning a retreat is to select the leadership. The two key people are the Retreat Coordinator and the Program Coordinator (see chapter 7). If fewer than 50 women attend your women's ministry, these two jobs could be done by one woman.

These leaders must be detailed-oriented and organized. Spiritual maturity is the primary ingredient when enlisting women for these key positions. Are they women of the Word and prayer? Can they keep confidences? Do they have the discernment to select speakers and oversee programming? Do they have a heart for the women?

Retreat Coordinator Responsibilities

- Is responsible to the women's ministry council coordinator.
- Meets regularly with the retreat program coordinator for prayer and the planning of the retreat.
- Selects speakers, corresponds with them and arranges transportation.
- Determines retreat schedule.
- Appoints workshop leaders, if applicable.
- Selects music ministry team leader.
- Acts as emcee for retreat sessions: welcoming, leading in prayer and introducing keynote speaker.

Retreat Program Coordinator Responsibilities

- Acts as an assistant to the retreat coordinator.
- Handles publicity, brochures and printing.
- Secures retreat site, meeting rooms, meal service and all applicable details.
- Makes announcements during the retreat.
- Appoints key positions for the retreat leadership team.
- Coordinates all retreat meetings.

Retreat Leadership Team

In addition to the retreat coordinator and program coordinator, the following positions are usually found on a retreat team. In a small church, one woman could handle several responsibilities. In a large church, each leader might have an assistant or a team to help her.

Music/Worship Leader

- Is responsible for all retreat music and worship.
- Provides song lyrics for retreat program.
- Arranges for special music.
- Acts as the point person for all sound system and staging details.

Facilities Coordinator

- Assigns meeting rooms and arranges for set up.
- Works with the registrar to assign women to their rooms or cabins.
- Is available onsite for rooming changes, should they become necessary.
- Coordinates set up and cleanup.
- Is responsible for the keys to the facility.

Registration Leader

- Is responsible for all registration details.
- Makes copies, distributes and collects all registration forms.
- Enters information into a database.
- Turns money over to the council finance coordinator for deposit.
- Works with the facilities coordinator to assign rooms to registrants.

Finance Team Leaders

To maintain a checks-and-balances system for the funds, it is suggested that there be two people responsible for finances for the retreat: one person responsible for the incoming fees and one person for the outgoing payments.

- Work with the retreat director to determine the budget for the retreat.
- Keep an account of all funds, incoming and outgoing.
- Keep all receipts and expenditures in a file to report after the retreat.

Prayer Team Leader

- Enlists women to form a prayer team that prays specifically for the retreat.
- Plans meetings with her team to pray for the retreat during the planning stages.
- Divides the names of the women on the registration list among the team members to pray for each woman prior to the retreat.
- Leads the team to pray for women at the retreat site, should the need arise.

Encouragement Team Leader

- Enlists women to form an encouragement team.
- Delegates encouragement team members to write and send notes to the women registered for the retreat, encouraging them on their decision to attend the retreat and letting them know that they are being prayed for as the retreat approaches.

Hospitality Team Leader

The hospitality team members are the warm smiles that women first see when arriving at the retreat. One woman should be designated as the team leader.

- Be the go-to women for questions or for help throughout the retreat.
- Stay updated on retreat particulars once onsite.

- Help out in the workshop rooms, discussion groups and any other activities where extra help might be needed.

Activities Team Leader
- Plan special outdoor activities, such as hikes, sports, tours or swimming.
- Plan indoor activities, such as pajama parties, crafts, game night and karaoke.

Entertainment Team
- Plan ways to help women feel comfortable through crowd breakers, community builders and skits.
- Coordinate entertainment with the retreat theme.

Hospitality Team Leader
- Chooses the gifts that the women will receive at the retreat (e.g., shirts, bags, cups, books).
- Orders and assembles gift bags and/or door prizes.

Food Team Leader
If you are providing your own meals at the retreat, this team would also be responsible for planning, shopping, cooking and cleanup.
- Organizes all snacks and makes sure there are enough finger foods in a common area.
- Makes food assignments if attendees are bringing food to the retreat.
- Is responsible for cleanup and storage of the food during the retreat.

Decoration Team Leader
- Plans all decoration details, theme tie-ins, sets or stage displays.
- Arrives early at the retreat site to set up decorations.

Graphic Designer
- Creates a logo around the retreat theme.
- Designs name tags, the program and handouts.
- Arranges for the printing of all materials with the approval of the women's council coordinator and the retreat coordinator.

Book Sales Coordinator
- Oversees the speaker's book table and/or women's ministry book table.

Newcomer Welcome Team
- Plans a preretreat welcome coffee or tea for the women new to the church or ministry.
- Helps new women find carpool partners to the retreat, answers any questions and goes out of the way to make the newcomers feel welcome.
- If budget allows, also arrange for special gifts to be given to each new woman (could be as simple as a bookmark).

Tips to Getting Started
- Cover the retreat in prayer.
- Secure a facility with good seminar rooms, guest rooms and a banquet room.
- Complete the facility contract.
- Secure a speaker.
- Determine a dollar amount to charge the retreat attendees based on room rate and food prices, and to cover all costs including speaker, hospitality gifts and snacks.
- Begin basic planning: Have a brainstorming session to develop a theme. This should probably be separate from your annual planning session, but you could do an initial plan at that time, i.e., set dates and location. Choose a color and design theme, and contact a graphic designer for brochure and program design. Follow a monthly timeline to keep things on track.

THE PLANNING SCHEDULE

For a successful retreat, begin planning far in advance. How far depends on the size of the group. The larger the group the more time needed to plan the details.

Nine Months to One Year Before Retreat

1. **The date** should be scheduled at least a year in advance. Avoid dates near the beginning or ending of school or holidays. Try to pick a consistent time from year to year, such as the first week in March or the third week in October so that women can plan ahead.
2. **Site selection** should be secured a year in advance. Choose an accessible location with comfortable beds. A drive of one to two hours can make it feel like a true get-away weekend. If

staying at a retreat center, you will probably want to reserve the facility for that same weekend for the next year, before leaving or within a few weeks after the end of the current retreat. If you like the facility, hold on to your spot!

3. **The theme** should be chosen before deciding on the speaker. However, sometimes a speaker is a good source for theme ideas. Most speakers will have certain topics on which they focus. If you choose the speaker first, you can adjust the theme to match her topics.

4. **The speaker** should be contacted six months to one year in advance. Never choose a speaker unless you or someone you trust has heard her speak. If she has been referred to you, contact her and ask her to send an audiocassette or video. Keep in mind that the speaker sets the tone for the retreat, so choose prayerfully and wisely. Clarify fees and transportation costs up front. Confirm everything in writing. Ask for a bio and photo for advertising. When budgeting for a speaker, keep in mind that the speaker is the main spiritual food at your retreat. If you divide the speaker's honorarium by the three or four sessions in which she will speak, then divide each session by the number of women in attendance, you will quickly see that you are only paying a small amount per woman per session for spiritual food!

5. **Meals** and food details should be determined at this time. If the retreat center provides this service, select and confirm the menus. Ask for healthy meals. If meals are not provided, you will need a team of kitchen workers to plan the meals and prepare them during the retreat.

Six to Eight Months Before the Retreat

1. **Plan the schedule,** including the main sessions, travel time, rest time and any optional workshops or extra activities. Keep the women active but not busy. A common mistake is to create a schedule that is so busy that the women feel exhausted rather than refreshed. Be sure to plan some optional activities so that each woman can choose those activities that suit her interests and physical abilities.

2. **Choose team leaders.** A leader is needed for each of the positions listed on pp. 99-101. All leaders must have a team mind-set. No woman should be an island, trying to do everything by herself.

3. **Choose workshops and workshop leaders,** if applicable. Plan to have a variety to choose from that will cover a broad spectrum—from home decorating to fasting, from the practical to the spiritual.

4. **Choose a music/worship leader.** If you are planning to bring outside musical talent, they should be reserved now. Just as with the speaker, ask for an audiocassette or a video to ensure a quality performance.

5. **Establish a budget** (see Budget Worksheet at the end of this chapter).
   - Estimate the total cost, including speaker fees, promotion, facility rental, food and decorations.
   - Determine the cost per person by dividing retreat expenses by the estimated number of women who will attend.
   - Get budget approval from the women's ministry council coordinator and the women's ministry financial coordinator.

Three Months Prior to the Retreat

1. **Promotion**—Begin promoting the retreat by gradually building excitement. Strive for excellence in your publicity.

2. **Printing**—Design and print the brochure. Include directions, speaker bio, information about retreat and the registration form. At this time make any posters or publicity that will be necessary for your retreat marketing. Artwork from the brochure can be made into a poster fairly easily at any copy-service facility.

3. **Registration**—This must be handled carefully. The opening registration date should be publicized well in advance. If it is likely to sell out, either make the retreat larger or have a set date and time to register on a first-come-first-served basis; then have a waiting list in case some attendees cancel. Establish the registration procedures ahead of time to avoid misunderstandings.

Two Months Before the Retreat

1. **Room assignments**—Allow the women to choose roommates when registering by having a space on the registration form that allows for this. But if a woman has no roommate or cabin preference, she must be assigned one (see sample registration form at end of chapter).

2. **Music**—A month before the retreat, the music/worship leader should give the lyrics to all group songs being used to the graphics artist to place in the printed program. Make sure all solos have been selected and approved. If planning a retreat theme song, make sure it is noted and highlighted.

3. **Skits**—Choose/plan skits and casts; conduct rehearsals.

4. **Prayer**—The prayer team leader should schedule regular prayer meetings to pray for the retreat and to assign names of registrants to specific prayer warriors.

5. **Food**—All food service, whether simply having snacks or preparing all of the meals, should be planned by this point.

6. **Facilities**—Contact site director to go over all details and tie up any loose ends.

7. **Gifts**—Order all hospitality gifts and gifts for the new women.

8. **Mailers**—Send letters to all registrants welcoming the women and providing a map to the retreat and information on the workshop options and free-time activities so that the attendees can be thinking about what they would like to choose. The letter should also have a number to call for questions, cancellations and carpool information.

9. **Prizes**—If including door prizes, collect them at this time.

Two Weeks Before Retreat

1. **Programs**—Print programs.

2. **Speaker**—Contact the speaker and the music performers to make sure they are well informed and have everything they need.

3. **Entertainment**—Check with the music/worship leader and the entertainment team leader to make sure everything is in place.

The Week of the Retreat

1. **Prayer Meeting**—It is essential to hold a prayer meeting the week of the retreat. Invite all the women involved in the retreat for a prayer time. If possible, have someone also lead in worship. Cover every aspect of the week in prayer.

2. **Gift Bags**—Have the hospitality team put together a gift bag for each attendee with a program booklet, a gift (e.g., shirt, mug or similar item), a pen/pencil, notebook, small tissue pack and a pack of gum or mints.

3. **Food Shopping**—The food team shops for all food items needed during the retreat.

4. **Speaker Gift**—The retreat coordinator or someone she delegates prepares a speaker basket that should include all the items you are giving the attendees plus several bottles of water, a few snacks and a special item chosen just for her. Include a card thanking her for coming to your retreat. If possible, have this waiting in her room, along with some fresh flowers.

5. **Phone Calls**—The retreat coordinator calls each lead team member and makes sure all is in place. She also asks if the leader needs prayer, has concerns or needs any help.

6. **Needs Basket**—Leaders should put together a "women's needs" basket that is kept in the main meeting room. It would include anything a woman might need but forgot—toothpaste, toothbrush, toiletries, Band-Aids, nail file, headache medicine, allergy medicine, eye drops, nose drops or feminine hygiene products.

7. **Focus**—Be flexible, but stay focused on the purpose. This retreat is not primarily about women; it's about Jesus and His desire to minister to the women in your group. Stay focused.

The Day of the Retreat

Finally, the long-awaited weekend arrives. The detail lists have been checked off, but things will still come up as you drive to the retreat center. Stay focused and flexible. Fix your mind on serving others for the weekend. Go prepared to serve as you lead, love and look out for the needs of others and any way you can help them. Smile and reach out (there's nothing worse than grumpy and unfriendly leaders).

Here are a few more last minute details to consider:

- Have team leaders arrive at the retreat location well in advance of the official starting time.
- Gather together as a team for prayer.
- Give out team instructions and assignments.
- Allow each team to do their own thing, preparing whatever needs to be finished by the time women arrive.
- Relax and wait for the women; be ready to greet them with kindness and a smile. This goes much further than you can imagine.
- Expect great things from God![2]

Follow Up

In the days and weeks following a retreat, plan a debriefing meeting for the attendees. At that time, review with the women what was taught, and if they were given a challenge or assignment, ask how they are doing. Also ask them to complete an evaluation form (see p. 112) to help in planning future retreats.

The follow-up could be done as part of a regular meeting or it could be a planned get-together just for those who attended. The leaders of the retreat could also write an encouraging note to each woman, reminding her about the theme and any challenges or projects that were suggested. Enclose an evaluation form with the note and ask the women to return the completed form at the next meeting.

If any women accepted Christ (or made a new commitment), be sure to follow up by pairing the new believer with a mentor or a small group to help her grow in her new relationship with Christ.

It is also a good idea to have a debriefing meeting for the retreat leadership team. Have them complete an evaluation form (see p. 111) and then discuss the comments on the attendees' forms and the leaders' forms. This would be a good time to begin planning for next year's retreat.

Notes

1. Carol Porter and Mike Hamel, eds., *Women's Ministry Handbook* (Colorado Springs, CO: Cook Communications, 1992), p. 162.
2. For additional retreat activity and craft ideas, refer to *Crafts and Activities for Women's Ministry* (Ventura CA: Gospel Light, 2004).

SAMPLE RETREAT SCHEDULE

Friday

4:30 P.M.	Arrivals and check-in
6:00-7:45 P.M.	Dinner in the dining hall
8:00 P.M.	Session One
10:00 P.M.	Snack time and games

Saturday

8:00-8:45 A.M.	Breakfast
9:00 A.M.	Session Two
10:45 A.M.	Break
11:00 A.M.	Panel discussion
11:30 A.M.	Workshop One
12:30 P.M.	Lunch
1:30-5:30 P.M.	Free-time activities: crafts, sports, shopping or hiking
5:30-5:45 P.M.	Welcome-back mixer
6:00 P.M.	Dinner in the dining hall
7:15 P.M.	Session Three
9:30 P.M.	Break
9:45 P.M.	Miniconcert with music team

Sunday

8:00- 9:00 A.M.	Breakfast in the dining hall
9:15 A.M.	Session Four, part 1
9:40-10:40 A.M.	Workshop Two
10:45 A.M.	Session Four, part 2
12:10 P.M.	Retreat wrap-up
12:15-1:00 P.M.	Lunch
1:30 P.M.	Adios!

Have a safe trip home!

Registration for Women's Spring Retreat
May 2, 3 and 4

Name _____

Address _____

City/Zip _____

Home phone _____

Work phone _____

Cell phone _____

E-mail _____

LODGING
❑ **Cabins**—$130
All scholarships will be economy accommodations
❑ **Select**—$145
❑ **Deluxe**—$165

A $50.00 nonrefundable registration fee is included in the room fee

To better serve special needs, please complete:

❑	Medical condition (please describe)
❑	Physical limitations
❑	I am interested in helping with this retreat. Area of interest:

To accommodate your bedtime and noise-level preference, please check your approximate time for lights out

❑ 10:30 P.M.   ❑ By 12:00 MIDNIGHT   ❑ After 12:00 MIDNIGHT

Room Key Deposit—Bring two $1 bills

❑ I am new to Cornerstone Fellowship.	❑ I wish to donate $ _____ toward the scholarship fund.
❑ I am in need of financial assistance.	❑ I wish to share a room with
	Name _____
In case of emergency, your services may be required.	Name _____
❑ I am CPR trained.	Name _____
❑ I have first-aid training	Name _____
	(Be sure your roommates list you on their form too.)

No refunds after April 13

Registration is from February 23 - April 17
Please return your registration form to the
Women's Ministries Table on Sundays,
midweek Bible studies or to the Church Office
during regular office hours.
Full payment is due by April 17

OFFICIAL USE ONLY

Paid ❑   Check/Number _____
                         ❑ **Cash**

Total Amount Paid $ _____
Scholarship Needed $ _____
Scholarship Donated $ _____
Accommodations $ _____

SAMPLE ACCOMMODATION DESCRIPTIONS

Accommodations

Cabins—Bunk beds (four to eight bunks per room) with a private bathroom; sleeping bag or linens needed.

Select—Separate rooms with private bath (some rooms sleep two; others sleep three), twin beds, linens and towel provided.

Deluxe—Private room with private bathroom; rooms have queen bed or twin beds. Linens and towels provided. Wheelchair accessible.

SAMPLE BULLETIN ANNOUNCEMENT

Women's Retreat Registration

Registration begins next Sunday, February 23, for our annual Spring Women's Retreat. This year's retreat theme is "Seasons of the Heart," with guest speaker Judy Hampton. It will be held May 2-4, at Redwood Christian Park in the Santa Cruz Mountains. Register at the women's ministry table on Sundays or at the midweek Bible study on Wednesdays or in the church office. This popular event fills up fast, so register soon.

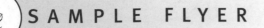

IT'S THAT TIME OF YEAR AGAIN!

CAN YOU BELIEVE IT?

May 2 to 4 Will Be Here Before We Know It!

Women's Spring Retreat Start-Up Meeting

Monday, January 6
7:00 P.M.
Fellowship Center
Room 204

If you have any interest in chairing or serving
on a committee, please come brainstorm with us.

Financial Assistance Request Form

Name _____ Today's Date _____

Address _____

Phone _____

Are you a regular attendee of Women's Ministry activities? ❑ Yes   ❑ No

How long have you been involved at the church? _____

Event requested for _____

What circumstances lend to your request for financial assistance?

_____

_____

_____

Payment Options

❑ I can pay the registration fee of $ _____today.

❑ I can contribute $ _____ toward the cost of the activity.

❑ I can contribute $ _____ per month over the next _____ months.

❑ I cannot afford payments beyond my registration fee.

❑ I cannot afford any payments and will need full financial assistance.

The above information is accurate and I agree to fulfill the above payment obligations in a timely manner. I understand that requests will be evaluated by an administrator on a case-by-case basis.

Signature _____

Date _____

Note: The information in this application will be held in strictest confidence.

Event Accounting Worksheet

Name _____ Today's Date _____

Ministry _____

Event _____ Event Date _____

Budget or Actual (circle one.)

Income		Outflow	
Registration fees		Deposits	
Donations		Facility payments	
Fund-raising		Speaker fees	
Scholarships		Publicity	
Book sales		Book costs	
		Musicians fees	
		Staff costs	
		Transportation fees	
		Printing brochures	
		Decorations	
		Hospitality	
		Food	
		Activities	
		Mailing costs	
		Entertainment costs	
Total Income		Total Expenses	

Net Income or <Loss>

$ _____

LEADER'S EVENT EVALUATION

Name _____ Date _____

Event _____

Area of Responsibility _____

What were the most significant activities at the event?

What weaknesses or problems did you see at the event?

What did you learn about being a leader?

What follow-up is needed (e.g., notes of encouragement, phone calls, meetings)?

Any suggestions for future similar events? (Use the other side of this page if you need more space.)

Thank you for your leadership for this event. May God continue to strengthen your relationship with Him and bless you for the time you gave to make it happen.

PARTICIPANT'S EVENT EVALUATION

Name (optional) _____ Date _____

Event _____

What were the most significant activities for you? Please explain your answer.

What weaknesses or problems did you see at the event?

What did you learn from this event?

Would you be willing to help with our next event? What talents, skills or abilities could you share with us?

Any suggestions for future events?

Thank you for your honest evaluation of this event. May God continue to strengthen your relationship with Him.

chapter fifteen

Reaching Women
THROUGH SPECIAL EVENTS

The LORD watches over all.

PSALM 145:20

Like retreats, special events can be the highlight of any ministry year. These events draw women who might not otherwise participate in church activities to a place where they can enjoy fellowship and hear the good news of Jesus Christ. These events also provide an opportunity for many women to serve in different areas. Some examples of special events include the following:

· Ladies' night out
· Christmas dinner
· Seminar day
· Heart groups

Chapter 13 provided descriptions of these special events. In this chapter we will look at a sample of each event and a planning model to help you get started with your own special events.

PLANNING TEAMS

Every event must be well planned. The following describes the coordinators and teams you may want to have for each event. These positions could be filled by the corresponding positions on the women's ministry council, or they could be short-term assignments just for the purpose of planning a specific event. Short-term assignments are a great way to get more women involved and to train future women's ministry leaders.

· **Coordinator** chairs the entire event and is responsible for choosing the speaker and for leading the special event team. She might also act as the emcee, or she can delegate that task to another women gifted at being in front of a group. She is responsible for pulling the event together through planning meetings and for delegating tasks as appropriate.

· **Activities/Entertainment Coordinator** leads the team that plans and organizes the activities for the event. These activities might include skits, outside entertainment, games, crafts and/or ice breakers. The activities team would also be responsible for acquiring and distributing door prizes or prizes for game winners.

· **Decorations Coordinator** chairs the team that puts together stage, room and table decorations based on the theme of the event. The decoration team is responsible for setting up the facility.

· **Publicity Coordinator** plans and carries out all advertisement for the event, provides printed materials and announces the event to other groups and the rest of the church family.

· **Music/Worship Coordinator** is responsible for providing special music or worship music for the event.

- **Food Team** plans the food and beverages that will be served and makes all necessary arrangements for the set up of the food tables. This team also provides paper products and might be responsible for decorating the food table in coordination with the decorating team. This team would also be responsible for preparing and serving the food if a caterer is not hired.
- **Set-Up Team** arrives early to help the decorations team with any set up.
- **Cleanup Team** stays after to take down all the decorations and to clean up, leaving the facility spotless.
- **Greeters/Hostesses** greet the women as they arrive, answer questions and direct the traffic flow.
- **Treasurer** is responsible for the registrations and for collecting the money for the event. She must keep accurate records and work in cooperation with the women's ministry finance coordinator.

The following pages outline some sample events to get you started. Each event will need most if not all of the coordinators and teams that are listed above.

LADIES' NIGHT OUT

This event can be held quarterly—either midweek or on a Friday night—depending on your demographics. It should have its own identity within the women's ministry with its own logo and planning team. A ladies' night out is a great summer get-together or perhaps a good cure for the winter doldrums.

Purpose

The purpose of a ladies' night out is to provide a night of inspiration, fun and fellowship to which women can invite guests, neighbors, coworkers and friends. The key to this event is to help develop relationships and provide an introduction to the Church and the gospel in a relaxed setting.

Planning

These ladies' nights out are placed on the church calendar when the women's ministry council plans for the year. A team specifically dedicated to these quarterly events should be selected at least three months before the event.

> **Note:** Since this is an outreach event, an information table should be prominently displayed with other women's ministry information such as newsletters, brochures and upcoming event publicity.

Date and Time

Wednesday, July 21 from 7:00 to 9:00 P.M.

Ticket Sales

Tickets will go on sale Sunday, June 20 and will cost $5.00 per woman.

Theme

Life's a Beach

Decorations

Decorate room in beach theme, using surfboards, beach balls, umbrellas, etc.

Music

Have Beach Boys or Hawaiian music playing as women enter and mingle.

Greeters

Greet each woman with a lei as she enters the room. Greeters should wear Hawaiian attire and leis. All team members should be dressed to fit the theme.

Food

Fruit cups with small drink umbrellas in them. Also provide punch, iced tea and cookies.

Program

6:45-7:25 P.M.	Women arrive and mingle. A greeting table should be located near the entrance, and hostesses should encourage women to get a name tag. Food and beverages are available.
7:25	Welcome from the coordinator (or emcee) who is dressed to fit the beach theme.
7:30	Skit related to the theme
7:45	Ice breaker—Beach Ball Toss: Women toss around several beach balls while the Beach Boys' classic "Wipe Out" is playing. Have two of the balls specially marked so that the women who end up with one of those balls wins a door prize. Door prizes could be manicure or pedicure gift certificates, a spa treatment, a massage or something similar.
7:55	Guest speaker incorporates the "Life's a Beach" theme, relating everyday challenges to a day at the beach and inspiring women to trust God with the challenges they face in their lives.
8:50	Music team closes the evening with special songs. These can be fun oldies and/or worship music.
8:55	Coordinator wraps up, announces the next women's event and closes in a prayer of blessing for the women.

COMMUNITY CHURCH WOMEN'S MINISTRY PRESENTS

Ladies' Night Out Summer Break

with special guest

CYNTHIA BECKMAN

Cynthia is a singer, songwriter and performer who shares her talent and spirit in concert and worship leading at special events all over the United States. Her desire is to share the grace and love of Christ with believers and seekers. Bring your friends and join us for an evening of fellowship, inspiration and fun.

Wednesday, July 21

Fellowship Room

7:00 P.M.

Enjoy a night of fun, fellowship and inspiration.
Wear your summer togs. Cost is $5.00 per person.

Please sign up by Sunday, July 18. Bring your friends too!

CHRISTMAS DINNER

The Christmas Dinner should be very festive and appropriate for outreach. Invite women to sign up in October to host a table of eight. The hostess decorates each table complete with a centerpiece, Christmas plates and a small gift for each woman. Some hostesses might sign up to set a table and then invite non-Christian women to be their guests.

Purpose

The purpose of the Christmas event is to usher in the holiday season with a specific focus on the reason for the season—the birth of our Savior and Lord, Jesus. This evening will hopefully provide a place of inspiration for those who dread the holiday season. This is an opportune time of year to reach unbelievers with the message of Jesus Christ and receptivity is very high for attending holiday gatherings.

Planning

This event should be put on the church calendar for the first week of December each year. This is a key outreach event and attention should be given to the program, speaker and music.

The Christmas Dinner Planning Team should be selected at least three months before the event is to be held and the planning should begin immediately. The menu will need to be decided early so that if a caterer is hired, you will be able to find one that has the date open. In lieu of a full dinner, you could simply serve a dessert.

Note: Since this is an outreach event, you might provide a Christmas store offering small items such as advent calendars, candles, Christmas albums, devotionals and books that will enhance the women's spiritual journey during the season. Another idea is to print up your own advent devotional for the women to use with their families or for personal enrichment. Women can shop on their way in or on their way out. The women's ministry's December (or quarterly) newsletter should also be made available for each woman in attendance. If you do not have a newsletter, at least provide a list of upcoming events and contact information for each event.

CHRISTMAS DINNER PLAN

Date

Friday, December 1

Tickets

Tickets go on sale November 1.

Publicity

Publicity should include advertisements in the church bulletin and printed brochures and postcards to mail. Remember that women should be encouraged to invite their unchurched friends, coworkers and relatives. This should be a major outreach.

Theme

The Perfect Gift

Decorations

These might include large, elegantly wrapped gift boxes, Christmas trees, white lights, candles and garlands. The individual tables can be beautifully decorated like a parade of tables. The attendees will enjoy seeing the different decoration ideas.

Music

Have carolers in traditional outfits singing as the women enter the room. The singers can carol throughout the room as the women view the decorated tables. Have instrumental Christmas music playing during the meal and special music planned for the program.

Greeters

Women are greeted and then directed to a hostess who helps them find their assigned table.

Food

Provide a catered dinner and an elegant dessert.

Program

6:30 P.M.	Doors open.
6:30-7:00	Women mingle, view tables and are served appetizers. Carolers sing around the room.
7:00	Carolers take the stage and open with one song.
	Emcee welcomes the women and makes announcements.
	Coordinator prays for the meal.
7:10	While Christmas music plays in the background, dinner is served.
7:50	Carol medley sing-along, concluding with a solo from the worship team.
8:10	Speaker talks about the perfect gift of Jesus.
9:00	Special music solo performed.
9:15	Emcee prays for a special blessing, thanks the women for attending and then bids the women good night and a merry Christmas.

Women's Ministry Christmas Dinner

Friday, December 1

Table Hostess Guidelines

Thank you for signing up to be a table hostess for our women's ministry Christmas dinner. This year's theme is "The Perfect Gift." We will kick off our holiday season by focusing on the reason for the season—Jesus. Once again, we will be at the Fellowship Center and Good Food Catering will pamper us with a wonderful celebration buffet.

All tables must be completely set and ready for guests no later than **5:00 P.M.** on December 1. You may begin setting your table as early as **2:00 P.M. As a table hostess, you have been given a number that will correspond with your table at the event.** A member of the event-planning team will be available to help you locate your table when you arrive. This year the doors will open to guests at 5:45 P.M., providing time for the women to view the tables and locate their seats. Our annual Christmas Dinner program will start at 6:30 P.M.

So what exactly am I supposed to do? **Great question!**

1. Please set your table (60 inches in diameter) for eight guests, including yourself. The table, chairs and a white tablecloth will be provided. The rest is up to you and your creativity. If you want to enlist a friend to help you—go for it! If you have invited guests to sit at your table, please reserve their places ahead of time; we have red "Reserved" cards if you wish to use them. We will also provide green "Available" cards for the place settings that are still vacant. Special greeters will seat those who do not have prior arrangements.

2. You are responsible for bringing your own dishes, silverware, glasses, napkins and centerpieces. Here are some ideas to help spice up your table: holiday tablecloth, placemats, candles and party favors or gift mementos. You may bring in anything you want to make your table festive, excluding alcoholic beverages. Our goal is for the women who attend to feel special and loved. Remember, this is not a contest; we simply want every table to be unique and beautiful. Some will be elegant, while others will be fun. Some will be colorful and some will be subdued, but each one will be a blessing to behold!

3. At the conclusion of the program, please completely clear your table. Out of respect for the speakers and guests, we request that the plates not be cleared until the end of the evening. We recommend that you bring a large laundry basket or other container to transport everything home. Your understanding and cooperation is greatly appreciated.

Thank you for participating in this event, sharing yourself with the women at your table and serving the women in our community by touching their lives with your love for Jesus. Please do not hesitate to call one of us should you have any questions or concerns.

If you have child care needs during the set up time, please call 555-2323 by November 20. We hope you enjoy the evening and are refreshed as we celebrate the birth of Jesus together.

TABLE HOSTESS APPLICATION

The Perfect Gift
Women's Christmas Event

Friday, December 1

Name _____

Home Phone _____ Cell _____

Work Phone _____

E-Mail Address _____

Please check the statement that applies.

❑ My table is full. I'm inviting seven guests.

❑ I am a table hostess, but I am not inviting guests; seven seats are available.

❑ My table will have _____ seats available for women.

The Event Center will open at 2:00 P.M. for table decorating. Tables will be numbered—your number appears at the bottom of this page. All tables must be completely set up by 5:00 P.M. Doors open to all guests at 5:45 P.M. for table viewing. Child care during setup is available by reservation only and is limited. Please contact _____ at _____ by November _____.

I have read the attached Hostess Guidelines. Enclosed is my payment of $_____ for my ticket.

_____

Signature   Date

Thank you so much for being a part of this wonderful Christmas tradition.

YOU HAVE BEEN ASSIGNED TABLE NO. _____.

SEMINAR DAY

This is a one-day retreat held at the church. This event could be planned in September to kick off the program year. If this is a kick-off event, provide information and registration for all ministries that will be offered this year.

One-day seminars could also be held at different times of the year for teaching the women in the church and helping them bond with each other. One-day seminars could be a substitute for a weekend retreat, so personal interaction time is extremely important.

Purpose

The purpose is to teach, equip and encourage women on their spiritual journey and to set the theme for the women's ministry year.

Planning

Place this event on the church calendar well in advance. Five to six months before the event, the Seminar-Day Team should be selected and should immediately begin planning.

Seminar Day Plan

Date

First Saturday *after* Labor Day weekend from 9 A.M.- 5 P.M.

Tickets

Tickets go on sale one month prior to the event for $30.00 each. Publicize this event through the church bulletin and direct mail with professionally made brochures. You might consider advertising in the local paper and radio or TV stations.

Theme

A Renewed Heart

Decorations

The decorating theme is butterflies, including a large banner on the stage and large butterflies hung from key areas. The butterfly signifies new life in Christ.

Greeters

Women stationed at tables in the foyer greet and sign in the women who are preregistered. Have a separate table to register walk-ins. After checking in, the women are given the day's program and a name tag.

Food

Provide a continental breakfast, coffee breaks and box lunches.

Sample Program

8:30 A.M.	Doors open, registration begins
8:30-9:15	Continental breakfast, coffee and fellowship
9:15	Welcome
	Opening music
	Skit or group ice breaker
	Session 1—The Condition of a Woman's Heart
10:45-11:00	Break
11:00	Session 2—The Reflections of a Woman's Heart
11:45	Special solo
11:50	Lunch—Catered box lunches
12:45 P.M.	Gather in main auditorium for worship and introduction of workshops by workshop leaders.
1:15-2:15	Workshop 1—Six workshops to choose from
2:30-3:30	Workshop 2—Six workshops to choose from (same as above)
3:45	Gather in main auditorium for special music.
4:00	Session 3—The Renewal of a Woman's Heart
4:45	Closing
5:00	Dismissal

A Transformed Heart

A Transformed Heart

I will give them an undivided heart and put a new spirit in them; I will remove from them their heart of stone and give them a heart of flesh.

Ezekiel 11:19

Women's Ministry
Fall Seminar with
special guest Jan Coleman

Saturday, September 20
8:30 A.M.-3:30 P.M. in the Ministry Center

About Our Speaker
Jan Coleman

If you like to laugh, if you want to grow closer to God, you will love Jan Coleman. She is a gifted speaker who has a way of reaching out to every woman, embracing her where she's at and sending her off with inspiration to meet life's demands. Author of the best-selling book *After the Locusts: Restoring Ruined Dreams, Reclaiming Wasted Years,* Jan is vulnerable and transparent. She merges her own life's lessons with solid biblical insights that challenge you to reach your highest potential for God.

Special Entertainment
The Sunshine Girls

Please join us for a day of teaching, inspiration and fun. The day includes entertainment, worship, teaching and fellowship.

Cost: $30.00, includes continental breakfast and catered lunch.

HEART GROUPS

Heart groups are not a one-time special event, but they are an effective outreach. They consist of small groups of 6 to 10 women who meet together once a month. Many women in your own neighborhood probably wouldn't attend church or a Bible study, but they might attend a heart group.

Leadership

Each heart group will need a leader and a hostess. The leader will direct the activities, and the hostess will provide her home and light refreshment. In a large women's ministry, there should probably be a heart groups coordinator. In a small ministry, the women's ministry council coordinator or Bible study coordinator could coordinate the leaders and hostesses. See p. 126 for a sample recruitment letter.

Meeting Basics

In the last week of each month, each heart group leader is sent the heart group connection correspondence. This will give each leader time to reflect on the next month's theme. Each group follows the same format and uses the same passage(s) each month so that all the groups are discussing the same topic.

- Welcome women into your home.
- Provide a light snack and drinks.
- Encourage fellowship time as women arrive.
- After about 30 minutes, bring the whole group together.
- Open in prayer.
- Have the month's text read aloud.
- Read the Scripture passage in other translations if clarity is needed.
- Begin processing, asking questions and sharing answers.
- Exchange prayer requests.
- Close in a circle of prayer.

The following are samples of heart group lessons.

HEART GROUP CONNECTION

June 2005

Scripture Passage

The words of Jesus Christ

Do not judge, or you too will be judged. For in the same way you judge others, you will be judged, and with the measure you use, it will be measured to you. Why do you look at the speck of sawdust in your brother's eye and pay no attention to the plank in your own eye? How can you say to your brother, "Let me take the speck out of your eye," when all the time there is a plank in your own eye? You hypocrite, first take the plank out of your own eye, and then you will see clearly to remove the speck from your brother's eye (MATTHEW 7:1-5).

Have someone read the text aloud. Also read it in different translations or paraphrases.

Things to Note
- Things that are emphasized
- Things that are repeated
- Things that are related
- Things that are alike
- Things that are unlike
- Things that are true to life

Theme of the Passage
- How does this apply to your own life?
- Do you struggle with this?
- How can this truth be applied to real life?
- What do you think a hypocrite is?
- How do you classify judging?

Word Meanings
- **Judge:** To form an evaluation or make an assumption. How does this definition help you break down the idea here of judging others?
- **Hypocrite**: A person who wears a pretense of superiority

Heart groups meetings that occur close to a holiday can follow a holiday theme as illustrated in the following example:

HEART GROUP CONNECTION
NOVEMBER 2005

Theme

- Being blessed
- Being thankful

Discussion

Matthew 5:1-16

Identify who is blessed and how (i.e., the poor in spirit—the kingdom of heaven).

- To which of the blessings do you relate? Why?
- Does it feel like you are blessed when you are in any of these given situations? Explain.

Traditionally the Thanksgiving holiday signifies a time of year when we as a nation and as individuals reflect on the year, our lives and what we are thankful for. Let's do that now.

- What kind of year has it been for you?
- Where is your life at right now?
- For what are you thankful?

It's been a hard year. Many are discouraged or troubled about the future.

- How do we give thanks when life seems less than what we desire?

Philippians 4:4-13; 1 Thessalonians 5:16-18

There are steps to looking to God and thanking Him while we wait for things to get better.

- What are the steps to waiting on God?
- What is the promise of thinking about the good in our lives?
- What did Paul learn to have in every circumstance?
- Who gave him the strength to go on even when life was hard?
- How can we live out the principles found in these passages?

Brainstorm as a group: How can we be a blessing to others? Discuss practical ideas for blessing others. Choose one thing that you could do as a group to bless someone in need of encouragement.

Because heart groups are ongoing outreach meetings, the team is made up of leaders and hostesses rather than coordinators or decoration teams. This makes recruitment by the coordinator a very important factor. The following is a sample recruitment letter that can be sent to possible leaders (a similar letter would be crafted to recruit hostesses):

Dear Potential Leader,

I have prayerfully been considering the women in our church, praying that God would lead me to women who can serve. As you know, the church is growing as we see God working through His Holy Spirit. Our challenge is to keep women connected to one another. That's where you come in. I am asking you to pray about being a heart group leader.

What is a heart group? A heart group is a group of 10 women that meets once a month in a member's home. The group could meet mornings, evenings, weekends or weekdays. Each leader, with her group, will determine when her group will meet.

The purpose of the heart group is very specific: It is for sharing, praying and encouraging. It's not a Bible study, and no homework is assigned. Each heart group leader is given a monthly theme and Scripture passage. All the heart groups will be discussing the same topic each month.

The group should also allow time for fellowship, coffee and light refreshments. The leader will bring the group together for a time of sharing, praying and encouraging. The leader will open with a reading of the theme passage. Leaders encourage application of the Word of God to daily living as each woman shares how she may be struggling or she may share answered prayers. The meeting will close with prayer.

The goal of these groups is to have a place for women to connect with other women. These groups do not take the place of other ministries.

I personally think you would make a great heart group leader. Please pray about this, and if you are interested I would like you to come to an upcoming leaders information meeting. Please respond and leave a message with my assistant.

Blessings,

Women's Ministry Council Coordinator
Connecting women to God and one another

A FINAL NOTE ON SPECIAL EVENTS

Because each community has it's own flavor, each ministry and each special event should reflect Christ in a way that will minister to the women you want to serve. Outreach events are an important part of the Body life and another opportunity to reflect His love, ushering others into a relationship with Him.

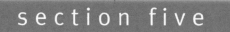
MAINTAINING
THE *Ministry*

chapter sixteen

Leadership BASICS

Ministry takes place when divine resources meet human needs through loving channels to the glory of God.

WARREN WIERSBE, *ON BEING A SERVANT OF GOD*

❧

Now that you have caught the vision and have begun serving the women of your church and community, what do you need to know about leadership? After catching a glimpse of what God wants you to do, it is easy to forget that it's all about Him. Leaders can also get so involved in their ministries that they forget that their position is *not* a one-woman show. Even in leadership, we must always remember that God called us to serve Him by serving others.

LEADERSHIP PRINCIPLES

There are four leadership principles that need to be restated often:

1. Remember Whom you are serving.
2. Remember why you are serving.
3. Remember what you have been called to do.
4. Remember that you achieve more with a team.

Whom You Are Serving

Serving God is a wonderful thing when we remember that God is doing the work in and through us. No matter how hard the work, we can keep going if we serve in the way that God tells us to in His Word. In his book *On Being a Servant of God*, Warren Wiersbe wrote:

> Certainly we need methods to serve God, but we must remember that methods work because of the principles behind that method . . . ministry is built on basic principles not clever methods. God doesn't want us to have ministry by imitation. He wants ministry by incarnation, what Paul wrote about in Philippians 2:13: "For it is God who works in you both to will and to do for His good pleasure."[1]

Ministry by imitation means copying the methods of others and trying to do things the same way they did. But ministry by incarnation means God is working in us and through us, often in ways unique to us or the ones we serve. Believe it our not, it is quite easy to leave God out of the equation of serving Him—doing ministry entirely through imitation and our own strength. This type of leadership does not bring glory to God—only credit to man. Contrarily, ministry by incarnation—or ministry in which God is working through us—is the type of work that brings glory and honor to the One we serve.

Wiersbe defined the four purposes of ministry as

1. To know the divine resources personally
2. To see the human needs compassionately
3. To become the channels of God's mighty resources
4. To glorify God alone in all we do— in our service to Him[2]

In remembering that we're serving God, we must put first things first, as covered in section 1 of this book. Memorize the following Scriptures to remember who we serve:

> Serve wholeheartedly, as if you were serving the Lord, not men, because you know that the Lord will reward everyone for whatever good he does (Ephesians 6:7-8).

> Whatever you do, work at it with all your heart, as working for the Lord, not for men, since you know that you will receive an inheritance from the Lord as a reward. It is the Lord Christ you are serving (Colossians 3:23-24).

Why You Are Serving

Why does God call people to leadership? To answer that question, we must know what a leader is and also discover the process of becoming a leader. To lead means "to guide or influence; to be a route or means to access."[3] Using this definition, we can see that we— as women serving other women—are not only an influence but also a connecting point. We are a means of access, a guide for bringing women along a road that encourages connection with Christ and friendships with other women.

A leader is defined as "a person or thing that leads; one that has the principal part in something; one whose example is followed."[4] With this definition in mind, we can see the importance in remembering the *why* of our service. We are not influencing people to buy a product, join a club or invest in a service. We

are, however, influencing people to turn their hearts and homes over to the living God. This is why, and it is the greatest privilege on Earth. Whether we are volunteering in the church or serving on church staff, the privilege is that we have the opportunity to be a part of the process that can lead women to Christ, and help them grow in their journey with Him.

Still the bottom line in our service is that God created us for Himself and to serve those around us. The following verses give foundation to that thought:

> For we are God's workmanship, created in Christ Jesus to do good works, which God prepared in advance for us to do (Ephesians 2:10).

> You did not choose me, but I chose you and appointed you to go and bear fruit—fruit that will last (John 15:16).

What You've Been Called to Do

Rick Warren wrote in his book *The Purpose-Driven Life*:

> Whenever God gives us an assignment, he always equips us with what we need to accomplish it. The custom combination of capabilities is called your SHAPE:
> - **S**piritual Gifts
> - **H**eart
> - **A**bilities
> - **P**ersonality
> - **E**xperience
> We have been shaped for serving God.[5]

The *what* in our service means that it is not about us! Rather our service is about something much grander than anything we could offer anyone. It is important to understand that God created each of us differently, equipping us ahead of time for the purpose that would be a part of our lives. It is important to keep our SHAPE before us, as we remember what we're called to. There are countless ministry ideas, visions and opportunities, but not every opportunity is right for us. We must always remember that it's about what Christ called us to—not what someone else expects of us. We must aim to serve in the context of God's plan for us! The following verses can remind us:

> I am the vine; you are the branches. If a man remains in me and I in him, he will bear much fruit; apart from me you can do nothing. If you remain in me and my words remain in you, ask whatever you wish and it will be given you. This is to my Father's glory, that you bear much fruit, showing yourselves to be my disciples (John 15:5,7).

> There are different kinds of gifts, but the same Spirit. There are different kinds of working, but the same God who works all of them in all men. Now to each one the manifestation of the Spirit is given for the common good (1 Corinthians 12:4,6-7).

Achieve More with a Team

Teamwork is an important concept to remember in leadership basics because God called us to work together and, in doing so, to be a part of the big picture.

Despite knowing we can't do it all, women are notorious for trying to do it all anyway. We are accustomed to multitasking and often feel it is easier to do something ourselves than to ask for help. Some of this attitude is in the favor of time efficiency—we believe that if we just do it without having to explain it, the job will get done quickly and easily. This cut-to-the-chase mind-set prohibits us from operating in God's kingdom the way he intended: as a unified team, a body and a family. The do-it-myself attitude might also come from our unspoken desire to control. Both of these attitudes cause us to remember the acrostic of **TEAM: Together Everyone Achieves More.** We must remember that we are called to serve with others.

As we come to understand our SHAPE for ministry, we will also find how we fit into the bigger picture, connecting link to link and dot to dot as we form a strong chain of united leadership. Though knowing our SHAPE is important, having a teachable heart and the heart of a servant is even more important. God created us with gifts and abilities so that we could serve Him effectively. He did not create us to be self-centered, and—let's face it—it's hard to operate as a team if we are each living solely for ourselves.

Few themes are clearer in the New Testament than the theme of love. Jesus always humbly underscored the importance of loving others. He lived His life on Earth as a servant—loving God and loving those around Him. He recruited a team of disciples at the beginning of His ministry. That team of 12 men did the work of the ministry and each one had his own part in the plan. Jesus chose these 12 men as His primary ministry group. In the context of His relationships with them, He taught them how to serve. Service is difficult in large groups and serving as a solo player depletes the Body of Christ of its unity. Warren Wiersbe wrote, "Here's a suggestion: build on your strengths, and ask God for helpers who can compensate for your weaknesses. Nobody's perfect, and nobody can do everything"[6].

John Maxwell verified this when he wrote, "Leaders don't focus on themselves and their own individual success. They think about the success of the organization and other people. They have an other-people mind-set. To develop others, you must teach them to think in terms of how they can promote others, develop others, take along others."[7]

Here's God's Word to match those thoughts:

> Just as each of us has one body with many members, and these members do not all have the same function, so in Christ we who are many form one body, and each member belongs to all the others. We have different gifts, according to the grace given us (Romans 12:4-6).

> But in fact God has arranged the parts in the body, every one of them, just as he wanted them to be. If they were all one part, where would the body be . . . (1 Corinthians 12:18-19).

Let's recap the four leadership basics:

1. Remember Whom you are serving.
2. Remember why you are serving.
3. Remember what you've been called to do.
4. Remember that you achieve more with a team.

Who? Why? What? With . . .

Notes

1. Warren Wiersbe, *On Being a Servant of God* (Nashville, TN: Oliver-Nelson, 1993), p. 2.
2. Ibid.
3. *Oxford American Dictionary,* s.v. "lead."
4. *Oxford American Dictionary,* s.v. "leader."
5. Rick Warren, *The Purpose-Driven Life* (Grand Rapids, MI: Zondervan Publishing House 2003), p. 236.
6. Warren Wiersbe, *On Being a Servant of God* (Nashville, TN: Oliver-Nelson, 1993), p. 26.
7. John Maxwell, *Developing the Leaders Around You* (Nashville, TN: Thomas Nelson Publishers, 1995), p. 205.

chapter seventeen

RECURUITING AND DEVELOPING
New Leaders

Professional organizations and businesses recognize the importance of selecting the right team—it should be no different in the Church. Too often people are placed in leadership positions haphazardly, finding later that they don't have the necessary giftings and skills; this can leave them frustrated, discouraged and even burned-out. When we do this in the Church, we are also setting ourselves up for trouble; it would be as if we were leading a group of people on a walk and everyone was wearing the wrong size shoes. And we all know how distracting an uncomfortable shoe can be: cramped, sore and blisteringly painful!

The following need to be considered when recruiting new leaders:

- What is needed in this ministry?
- Who do we already have serving who fits this need?
- Who is available to fill this need?
- Who is willing to serve in this way?
- Who is gifted and able to get things done?

Remember, filling a ministry position—even a volunteer position—is like skydiving: Once you've jumped out of the plane, you're committed! It's impossible to climb back up and start over again.

Here are 10 qualities to look for when recruiting leaders:

1. **Positive Outlook**—Has the ability to work with people and sees situations in a positive way.
2. **Servanthood**—Has the willingness to submit, work with a team and follow the leader.
3. **Growth Potential**—Has a hunger for personal growth and development along with the ability to grow as the ministry expands.
4. **Follow-Through**—Has the determination to get the job done completely and consistently.
5. **Loyalty**—Has the willingness to put the supervisor and the organization above personal desires.
6. **Resiliency**—Has the ability to bounce back when problems arise.
7. **Integrity**—Has a wide array of traits that include trustworthiness, solid character and consistent words.
8. **Big Picture**—Should have the ability to see the whole organization and its needs.
9. **Discipline**—Should have the willingness to do what is required regardless of personal mood.
10. **Gratitude**—Possesses an attitude of thankfulness that has become a way of life.[1]

When building ministry teams, it is important that you select people who believe in the vision and purpose statement of the ministry and the church. Select women who have a similar ministry philosophy and in whom you see potential. Then find out what they need. Do they need encouragement, skill training, objectivity?

Once the women are in a leadership position, give them regular feedback, especially as they develop and step out into new areas of ministry. Be sure that they have adequate training and direction in the area in which they serve. Giving clear directions goes much further than the initial recruitment and commitment. When a leader has a clear understanding of what is expected of her, she can get to work. As simple as that sounds, it goes a long way in strengthening your leaders. Providing clear directions can also help you when giving feedback, encouragement or evaluation because you can give them objective guidelines.

The following pages provide examples of detailed descriptions for different ministries and the types of leaders needed.

Women's Book Club

Purpose

To bring a group of women together to connect with one another and to God through the reading and discussion of books.

Meetings

The book club meets once a month at a bookstore, restaurant or home and lasts approximately an hour and a half.

Leadership Expectations

The club leadership will consist of one leader and a coleader. The expectations for each are as follows:

Leader

The club leader is expected to attend and lead discussion at the monthly book club meeting. She should arrive 10 minutes early and set out refreshments and name tags. The club leader is directly responsible to the women's ministry council coordinator or the small-groups coordinator.

Coleader

The coleader supports the leader. She reads the book each month and helps with organizational details: arriving early, bringing refreshments or filling in if the leader is unable to attend. The coleader is directly accountable to the leader.

Choice of Books

The leader is responsible for choosing books for the upcoming months and will present the book chosen for the next month at each meeting. The leader has the freedom to choose Christian books or literature approved by the women's ministry council coordinator. The leader can also choose seasonal themes if desired.

Sample Meeting Plan

- The meeting will be held in the bookstore café on the last Tuesday of the month from 7:00 to 8:30 P.M.
- The coleader will provide simple refreshments.
- Name tags will be provided by the leader.
- The leader will come prepared to lead an informal discussion of the current book, using a few lead-in questions.
- The leader will prepare several ice-breaker questions to get things going (see *Crafts and Activities for Women's Ministry* for ideas).
- If the group is large (more than 10 women), the group should be divided into two groups and the coleader will lead the second group.

Time Commitment

This is a volunteer position within women's ministries that will take approximately 10 hours a month, 10 to 12 times a year. The leader is asked to make a one-year commitment at the beginning of the program year. The group may elect to not meet one month during the summer and one month during the holidays. The leader will be directly accountable to the women's ministry council coordinator or the small-groups coordinator.

This position of ministry is valued and appreciated as it will help women who enjoy reading connect to each other and to God through purposeful fellowship. It is also a great opportunity to bless others and encourage them in their continued spiritual growth.

Pillars of Faith Ministry

Purpose

Provide support and encouragement to women who feel alone in their faith due to a marriage partner who is not a believer.

Theme Verse

"If any of them do not believe the word, they may be won over without words by the behavior of their wives" (1 Peter 3:1).

Mission

The mission of the Pillars of Faith Ministry is to encourage, pray and share with others who are in the same situation.

Meetings

This ministry meets once a month for discussion on specific topics and prayer. The group members might choose to do a Bible study together.

Leaders

This group is led by two coleaders who have committed for one year. The leaders should be prepared to lead discussions. There will not be any homework for the group, but the leaders will provide the spiritual format to get the group grounded and to keep it going.

Sample Meeting

- The meeting will be held in the church's Fireside Room on the last Tuesday of the month from 10:00 to 11:30 A.M.
- Hot and cold beverages will be served.
- The leaders will come prepared to lead a brief discussion based on a Scripture passage pertinent to the women's needs or on a specific topic, such as how to find fun activities to do with your unbelieving husband.
- The group will take specific prayer requests and pray for one another.

LEADERSHIP DEVELOPMENT

You have identified several key potential leaders, so now what? If they have agreed to join the team and you have outlined clear expectations and guidelines for their area of service, it's time for them to develop and grow in the areas to which they have committed.

The following is John Maxwell's five-step process for training people:

Step 1: Model

Do the tasks in front of those being developed and trained. Allow them a window into the whole process. Let them shadow a leader in the position. Too often when we train people we bring them in on the middle of a project and assume they get it. We need to walk through the ministry with them and before them. Don't just tell them how to do something—show them.

Step 2: Mentor

Continue to perform the work of the ministry, but this time the leader in training should come alongside and assist in the work. Explain how but also the why of each step.

Step 3: Monitor

The leader in training does the work of the ministry while they are assisted and corrected, if necessary, by the leader training her. Always remain positive and encouraging. Ask the leader trainee to repeat the steps and the process back to you.

Step 4: Motivate

Keep encouraging the young leader until she is ready to step out on her own.

Step 5: Multiply

Once the new leaders complete the job and do it well, it's their turn to teach and train others.[2]

LEADERSHIP DELEGATION

Ministries with leaders who can't delegate create a bottleneck to growth and creativity in ministry. Even though delegation is important for success, some leaders aren't able to bring themselves to delegate tasks and authority. A big reason for this is usually insecurity. Some leaders are afraid that if they aren't in control of everything, they aren't doing their job or that the job will not be done properly. This can be found in any area of ministry.

Do you have a retreat coordinator who has to be involved in every detail? To whom is she delegating? Is she comfortable trusting others to use their gifts? What is she communicating to her team by needing to be involved in everything?

Some leaders just don't know how to train or they don't want to take the time. Others don't train out of the habit of doing things themselves or out of a reluctance caused by past failures. Whatever the case, lack of delegation prohibits team building, and when we are not working as a team, we are not a Body joined together by Christ.

To continue developing new leaders, we must maintain a positive environment for growth and training, and a belief in the leaders around us by allowing their gifts to surface and take shape. The following characteristics are very important in any aspect of women's ministry—from handling registration for an event to teaching a Bible study—with the first two being the most important.

- Humility
- Teachability
- Positive attitude
- A heart for people
- People skills
- Giftedness and fruit bearing
- Established track record
- Confidence in God
- Growing relationship with Christ
- Self-discipline
- Good communication skills

Good leadership flows from women who cast vision, model character, encourage relationships with Christ and invest time in the people being served. Building a leadership team is challenging, but with Christ we can walk through the murky waters of leader discontent, program changes and leader conflicts.

In the meantime, stay on the lookout. Look for women who have a heart for God and a heart for women. Don't be afraid to approach them and ask if they are interested in serving God within the context of the women's ministry. Let them think it over; then follow up informally. Get to know each woman; ask questions about her life; ask questions about her relationship with God and about her background and experiences. Before long, you will see how easy it is to recruit leaders by discovering who they are and where they've been. With your help, they will get a glimpse of where they are headed as God's servant leaders.

Notes

1. John Maxwell, *Developing the Leaders Around You* (Nashville, TN: Thomas Nelson Publishers, 1995), p. 23.
2. Ibid.

chapter eighteen

DEALING WITH
Conflict

Let us therefore make every effort to do what leads
to peace and to mutual edification.

ROMANS 14:19

In his book *On Being a Servant of God*, Warren Wiersbe wrote:

> When our older daughter was a child in grade school, one day she came storming into the house, slammed the door, stomped into her room, slammed that door, all the while muttering under her breath, "People—people!—PEOPLE!" Thinking that I might be of some help, I tapped on the door and asked, "May I come in?"
> The answer was an explosive "No!"
> "Why?" I asked.
> "Because you're a people!"[1]

We all have problems with people. One thing's for sure: Believers who try to serve the Lord can expect to have problems with people, and they might find that people have problems with them!

It would be great if everyone always got along. But in the real world and in ministry, relationships are often in conflict. Within any and every women's ministry, conflicts and problems will arise. Even within the leadership team trouble will rear its ugly head from time to time. Know that there is a high proba-bility of conflict. But knowing isn't enough—we must be prepared for dealing with the tough stuff.

> Any kingdom divided against itself will be ruined, and a house divided against itself will fall (Luke 11:17).

Within the context of ministry, we need to take the team approach, encouraging support for one anoth-er. A conflict might be something as simple as a per-sonality clash or something as serious as a betrayal. On each end of the spectrum and at every point in between are women who want to be loved, valued and understood.

A ministry divided will fall. A person who divides a group is thinking only of herself and not of the wel-fare of the overall team and ministry.

CARE ENOUGH TO CONFRONT

Many people avoid confrontation. Some fear being disliked and rejected. Others are afraid confrontation will make things worse by creating anger and resent-ment in the person they need to confront. But when a person's behavior is inappropriate, avoiding con-frontation always worsens the situation. When a woman is acting inappropriately and isn't told about it, she is robbed of an important opportunity to learn and grow in her maturing process. Any time a leader avoids a confrontation, she should ask herself whether she is holding back for the good of the organization or for personal reasons. If a leader avoids confronting another person for her own well-being, that leader is acting under selfish motives.

We have been conditioned to believe that out of every conflict comes a winner and a loser. But that isn't necessarily true. To produce a win-win situation, we must approach confrontation with the right attitude. Think of confrontation as a chance to help the people involved to mature. Never confront while angry or to show power. Check your heart attitude before you confront and then confront with respect for the other person involved.

FOLLOW THE BIBLICAL PATTERN

If your brother sins against you, go and show him his fault, just between the two of you. If he listens to you, you have won your brother over. But if he will not listen, take one or two others along, so that every matter may be established by the testimony of two or three witnesses (Matthew 18:15-16).

The biblical pattern might work like this:

1. Go directly to the person with whom you are having a problem.
2. Calmly state your concern; then seek reconciliation and understanding.
3. If she is not receptive, meet with her again with a witness.
4. If she is still not receptive, bring it before the leadership team.

The longer you wait to confront someone, the more distracted you will be by the problem, and the problem may even grow worse as you delay the inevitable. The longer you are distracted, the less effective your ministry will be.

The following suggestions may help:

- Separate the person from the wrong action. Address the harmful action and confront it, not the person. Continue to affirm and encourage the person.
- Confront only what the person can change. If we ask a person to change something she can't, such as her talkative nature, she will become frustrated and it will strain your relationship.
- Give the person the benefit of the doubt. Always try to start with the assumption that a person's motives were right.
- Be specific. The person being confronted can only address and change what is specifically identified. If you can't identify specifics, there may be further misunderstandings.
- Avoid sarcasm because it indicates anger with people, not their actions.
- Avoid saying things like "You always" and "I never."
- Affirm her as a person and a friend. Prepare to confront in the same way you fix a sandwich. Put the confrontation in the middle, between affirmation and encouragement.[2]

Positive confrontation is a sure sign that you care for a person and have her best interests at heart. Each time you build up people and identify problems, you give them an opportunity to grow. In the process, you develop authenticity in ministry relationships. Authenticity is the quality of being genuine, real and true. If we aren't real with the others in leadership, the door will always be open for competition, phoniness and fake spirituality. This is not appropriate for those of us who are submitting to the call to follow Jesus. What steps can we take as leaders to move toward authenticity in our relationships?

Confess your sins to each other and pray for each other so that you may be healed. The prayer of a righteous man is powerful and effective (James 5:16).

Confessing your sins requires humility. Praying together restores unity.

DEVELOP UNITY

Be Merciful

Read the words of Christ from Luke 6:36-41:

Be merciful, just as your Father is merciful. Do not judge, and you will not be judged. Do not condemn, and you will not be condemned. Forgive, and you will be forgiven. Give, and it will be given to you. A good measure, pressed down, shaken together and running over, will be poured into your lap. For with the measure you use, it will be measured to you. . . . Can a blind man lead a blind man? Will they not both fall into a pit? . . . Why do you look at the speck of sawdust in your brother's eye and pay no attention to the plank in your own eye?

Let's recap what this verse is telling us.

- We will fall or fail to accomplish God's purpose when we are divided.
- We must learn to honestly assess ourselves first, looking for our own shortcomings, not the faults of others.
- We must look for the best in each other.
- When there is a problem, misunderstanding or offense, we must deal directly with the person with whom we have the problem instead of escaping to gossip and complaining to others.
- We must be merciful, open armed, comforting, caring and loving.
- We must learn to be giving.

Love Sincerely

Love must be sincere. Hate what is evil; cling to what is good. Be devoted to one another in brotherly love. Honor one another above yourselves (Romans 12:9-10).

As a leader, ask yourself the following questions:

- Are you a judgmental person?
- Do you measure others by your standards or by Jesus' standards?
- Do you find it difficult to look for the best in others and focus on the good?
- Do you have trouble with telling the truth about how you feel—especially when you have felt wronged or hurt?
- How do you react when someone confronts you about your behavior?
- What plank is in your own eye that needs prayer today?

A. W. Tozer once said, "Never be afraid of honest criticism. If the critic is wrong, you can help him; and if you're wrong, he can help you. Either way, somebody's helped."[3]

Those of us who serve Christ should strive to minister like Christ. He washed the dirty, stinking feet of 12 men who were unworthy of His presence, let alone His service. He received and helped multitudes of people, many of whom never accepted His message. He died for a world that doesn't want Him. Why did He do it? Because it was the Father's will.

Notes

1. Warren Wiersbe, *On Being a Servant of God* (Nashville, TN: Oliver-Nelson, 1993), n.p.
2. John Maxwell, *Developing the Leaders Around You* (Nashville, TN: Thomas Nelson Publishers, 1995), pp. 126-127.
3. A. W. Tozer, quoted in Warren Wiersbe, *On Being a Servant of God* (Nashville, TN: Oliver-Nelson, 1993) p. 52.

chapter nineteen

NETWORKING WITH OTHER
Ministries

Connecting with other women in ministry can refresh your vision, enhance your ideas and add more substance to the ministry programs at your church. Networking with other women's ministries in your area can also promote unity between churches as local women work together toward a Kingdom cause.

At its essence, networking forms a chain of connections between people of similar interests. Networking with other women's ministry teams can help you build a new ministry because they may have already worked out the kinks and can warn you of potential mistakes. Networking can energize an existing ministry by accomplishing more through shared ideas, connections and work load.

HOW DO I FORM A LOCAL NETWORK?

Call a few of the churches in your area and ask to speak to the person in charge of women's ministries. Inquire about women's ministry networking groups or meetings. If there are not any in your area, ask a few of the women's ministry coordinators you speak with if they are open to the idea of joining a women's ministry network.

Planning the First Meeting

- Determine which churches are in your area.
- Make a list of churches to invite.
- Choose a date, time and place to meet.
- Design an invitation to spark interest and encourage involvement.
- Contact everyone the week before the meeting.
- Create a meeting agenda (see the sample below).

The Meeting

- Greet each woman as she arrives.
- Have meeting agenda, name tags and pens available.
- Provide beverages and finger foods or dessert.
- Formally welcome everyone.
- Open in prayer.
- Have each women introduce herself and her ministry position.
- Share the vision of ministry networking.
- Share openly about your dreams and plans.
- State the date of the next meeting.
- Give out assignments for the next meeting.
- Close with prayer.
- Have information sheets available.

Assignments for the Next Meeting

Before the next meeting, ask the women to prepare the following:

- A suggestion for the mission statement for the networking group
- A suggestion for the purpose and theme verse
- Speaker ideas and reference lists
- Event ideas

The Fruit of Networking

The following story illustrates the fruit of networking:

It only took one local woman to act as a catalyst for bringing together women in leadership from 12 different churches. Though she didn't know what the response would be, she took a leap of faith by planning the first meeting and putting everything into action. The results were far beyond what she anticipated.

At the meeting, every woman expressed her desire to be involved, realizing the importance of being connected as the Body of Christ. The idea of unity, shared ideas and leadership fellowship was enticing to every woman present.

This group of 12 formed a mission statement and decided to launch their unified efforts by reaching out to the entire area in which they served. It was the year of the 9/11 tragedy, and they knew women were looking for answers and they knew women needed Christ.

Together they planned an areawide event that they called Valley Vision. Each woman went back to her local church for approval and support. Every pastor agreed to support the event and was encouraged by what these women were doing. The budget was entirely paid for by the ticket price for the event.

They spent months planning the event, renting a local hotel ballroom. The network got the news out to their worship teams and formed a Valley Vision team to incorporate the women from different churches. They found actors for skits and presenters through the network. They held prayer meetings in advance and experienced unity they had never seen before.

The first year they sold out the event and had over 1,200 women in attendance. The team encouraged women in local churches to bring one friend. It was exciting to see women jump on board quickly, inviting seekers and talking about the event throughout the area.

Since that initial event there have been more unity and team efforts among the valley churches. The next year they planned the second annual Valley Vision, which drew media coverage from the local TV stations and the local newspapers. This circle of ministry leaders from different churches with different backgrounds united for one specific reason—to exalt Jesus Christ in their community—and they have made a huge impact in their community.

Local Networks

The results of networking with local churches includes breaking down walls of pride and competition; encouraging fellowship and support between other churches; teaching women how to work in unity for a Kingdom cause; encouraging leaders to be community team players; developing new friendships and providing an example for those they serve and for other churches to work together in unity.

National Networks

There are also many other ways to network women's ministry leaders across the state or nation. There are a variety of websites that offer women's ministry ideas, tips and conferences. There are also women's ministry chat rooms and e-mail encouragement loops. With the presence of magazines and books available on the Internet, there are an amazing amount of resources at your fingertips. The appendix in this book contains lists of resources to aid you.

Taking your team to a national conference is also a good investment of ministry time and finances. You can provide for your team to attend by planning in advance and generating income through fund-raisers.

Women's
MINISTRY RESOURCES

SEMINARS AND CONFERENCES

Women's Ministries

Women of Faith
For more information about upcoming Women of Faith conferences, visit www.womenoffaith.com.

Living Proof Live
The Living Proof Live conferences feature Beth Moore, founder of Living Proof Ministries. For more information about the conferences and a conference schedule, visit www.lproof.org.

Right to the Heart of Women
Right to the Heart of Women provides support and encouragement to women of the Church, women's ministries and women in ministry. For more information about Right to the Heart of Women and their annual conferences, visit www.righttotheheartof women.com. For information about their leadership conferences, visit www.AttendNow.com.

Design for Living
For more information about Design for Living Ministries and its seminars, featuring founder Debbie Alsdorf, visit www.design4living.org.

Intimate Issues
The Intimate Issues conferences tackle the most common questions women have about intimacy issues, whether single or married. For more information, visit www.intimateissues.com.

Hearts at Home
Hearts at Home conferences exist to encourage and educate mothers at home. The Hearts at Home network also offers a magazine, devotionals, a website and referrals. Find more information at www.heart sathome.org.

Speakers

Advanced Writers and Speakers Association (AWSA)
AWSA is a network of the top Christian women writers and speakers. For a directory of AWSA members that includes their areas of expertise, visit www.AWSAwomen.com.

Christian Leaders, Authors and Speakers Services (CLASS)
CLASS is a complete service agency providing resources, training and promotion for Christian speakers, authors and publishers. For a complete list of speakers, along with their topics and booking information, or to find more information about their speaker training events, visit www.classservices.com.

Speak Up
Speak Up Speaker Services is a service agency that connects extraordinary Christian communicators with groups that need their services. Browse their database of more than 100 Christian speakers, which

includes their expertise and booking information, at www.speakupspeakerservices.com. For information about the three-day Speak Up with Confidence seminars, visit www.speakupspeakerservices.com/Seminars.asp.

Women's Ministry Network

Founded by author, speaker and recording artist Jennifer Rothschild, the Women's Ministry Network provides a newsletter, a women's ministry directory and a women's ministry event registry and is an excellent source for ideas, resources and information exchange among Christian women and ministry organizations. Find out more information at www.womensministry.net.

REFERENCE MATERIALS

Discipling New Believers

Alsdorf, Debbie. *My New Relationships in Christ.* Colorado Springs, CO: David C. Cook Publishing, 2003.

Baker, Julie. *My New Identity in Christ.* Colorado Springs, CO: David C. Cook Publishing, 2003.

McGuirk, Nancy. *My New Life in Christ.* Colorado Springs, CO: David C. Cook Publishing, 2003.

Leadership

Briscoe, Jill, Laurie Katz McIntyre, and Beth Seversen. *Designing Effective Women's Ministries.* Grand Rapids, MI: Zondervan Publishing House, 1995.

Erwin, Gayle. *The Jesus Style*, 3rd ed. Cathedral City, CA: Yahshua Publishing, 1997.

Farrel, Pam. *Woman of Influence: Ten Traits of Those Who Want to Make a Difference.* Downers Grove, IL: InterVarsity Press, 1996.

Nelson, Alan. *Spirituality and Leadership: Harnessing the Wisdom, Guidance and Power of the Soul.* Colorado Springs, CO: NavPress, 2002.

Porter, Carol, and Mike Hamel, eds. *Women's Ministry Handbook.* Wheaton, IL: Chariot Victor Books, 1992.

TerKeurst, Lysa. *Leading Women to the Heart of God: Creating a Dynamic Women's Ministry.* Chicago, IL: Moody Press, 2002.

Wiersbe, Warren. *On Being a Servant of God.* Grand Rapids, MI: Baker Book House, 1999.

Mentoring

Biehl, Bobb. *Mentoring: Confidence in Finding a Mentor and Becoming One.* Nashville, TN: Broadman and Holman, 1997.

Huizenga, Betty. *Apples of Gold: A Six-Week Nurturing Program for Women.* Colorado Springs, CO: David C. Cook Publishing, 2000.

Kraft, Vickie, and Gwynne Johnson. *Women Mentoring Women: Ways to Start, Maintain and Expand a Biblical Women's Ministry*, rev. ed. Chicago, IL: Moody Press, 2003.

Otto, Donna. *Between Women of God: The Gentle Art of Mentoring.* Eugene, OR: Harvest House Publishers, 1995.

Small-Group Resources

Donahue, Bill. *Leading Life-Changing Small Groups*, rev. ed. Grand Rapids, MI: Zondervan Publishing House, 2002.

Donahue, Bill, and Russ Robinson. *Building a Church of Small Groups.* Grand Rapids, MI: Zondervan Publishing House, 2001.

——.*The Seven Deadly Sins of Small Group Ministry.* Grand Rapids, MI: Zondervan Publishing House, 2002.

Galloway, Dale, and Kathi Mills. *The Small Group Book: The Practical Guide for Nurturing Christians and Building Churches.* Grand Rapids, MI: Revell, 1995.

Griffin, Em. *Getting Together: A Guide for Good Groups.* Downers Grove, IL: InterVarsity Press, 1982.

McBride, Neal. *How to Have Great Small-Group Meetings: Dozens of Ideas You Can Use Right Now.* Colorado Springs, CO: NavPress, 1997.

Ogden, Greg. *Discipleship Essentials: A Guide to Building Your Life in Christ.* Downers Grove, IL: InterVarsity Press, 1998.

Women's Issues

General

Barnhill, Julie. *She's Gonna Blow: Real Help for Moms Dealing with Anger.* Eugene, OR: Harvest House Publishers, 2001.

Newman, Deborah. *Loving Your Body: Embracing Your True Beauty in Christ.* Wheaton, IL: Tyndale House Publishers, 2002.

——. *A Woman's Search for Worth: Finding Fulfillment as the Woman God Intended You to Be.* Wheaton, IL: Tyndale House Publishers, 2002.

O'Connor, Karen. *Help, Lord! I'm Having a Senior Moment: Notes to God on Growing Older.* Ventura, CA: Regal Books, 2003.

——. *Professionalizing Motherhood*, exp. ed. Grand Rapids, MI: Zondervan Publishing House, 2002.

——. *Creating the Mom's Group You've Been Looking For: Your How-To Manual for Connecting with Other Moms.* Grand Rapids, MI: Zondervan Publishing House, 2004.

West, Kari. *Dare to Trust, Dare to Hope Again: Living with Losses of the Heart.* Wheaton, IL: Chariot Victor Publishing, 2001.

West, Kari, and Noelle Quinn. *When He Leaves: Choosing to Live, Love and Laugh Again.* Wheaton, IL: Chariot Victor Books, 1998.

Wright, H. Norman. *Always Daddy's Girl: Understanding Your Father's Impact on Who You Are.* Ventura, CA: Regal Books, 2001.

Healthy Living

Lewis, Carole. *Choosing to Change.* Ventura, CA: Regal Books, 2001.

Lewis, Carole, with Terry Whalin. *First Place.* Ventura, CA: Regal Books, 2001.

First Place. *First Place Leader's Guide.* Ventura, CA: Gospel Light, 2001.

——. *First Place Member's Guide.* Ventura, CA: Gospel Light, 2001.

——. *Giving Christ First Place.* Ventura, CA: Gospel Light, 2001.

> For more information about the First Place program and a complete list of products, call 1-800-4-GOSPEL or visit www.firstplace.org.

Russell, Rex. *What the Bible Says About Healthy Living: Three Biblical Principles That Will Change Your Diet and Improve Your Health.* Ventura, CA: Regal Books, 1996.

Intimacy

Dillow, Linda, and Lorraine Pintus. *Intimate Issues: Twenty-One Questions Women Ask About Sex.* Colorado Springs, CO: WaterBrook Press, 1999.

Savage, Jill. *Is There Really Sex After Kids?* Grand Rapids, MI: Zondervan Publishing House, 2003.

Bible Studies

Aglow Bible Study Series

Gibson, Eva. *Forgiveness.* Ventura, CA: Gospel Light, 1999.

Goodboy, Eadie. *A Woman After God's Heart.* Ventura, CA: Gospel Light, 1999.

Goodboy, Eadie, and Agnes Lawless. *God's Character.* Ventura, CA: Gospel Light, 1998.

Powers, Marie. *Shame: Thief of Intimacy.* Ventura, CA: Gospel Light, 1998.

Steele, Sharon. *Choosing to Change.* Ventura, CA: Gospel Light, 1998.

——. *Keys to Contentment.* Ventura, CA: Gospel Light, 1998.

——. *Loving As Jesus Loves.* Ventura, CA: Gospel Light, 1999.

Wise, Janice. *Walk Out of Worry.* Ventura, CA: Gospel Light, 1999.

Yagel, Bobbie. *Building Better Relationships.* Ventura, CA: Gospel Light, 1998.

Focus on the Family Women's Series

Focus on the Family. *Balanced Living.* Ventura, CA: Gospel Light, 2004.

——. *Healing the Heart.* Ventura, CA: Gospel Light, 2004.

——. *The Blessings of Friendships.* Ventura, CA: Gospel Light, 2004.

——. *Women of Worth.* Ventura, CA: Gospel Light, 2004.

Studies by Beth Moore

Moore, Beth. *Beloved Disciple: The Life and Ministry of John.* Nashville, TN: LifeWay, 2002.

——. *When Godly People Do Ungodly Things: Arming*

Yourself in an Age of Seduction, Member Book. Nashville, TN: LifeWay, 2003.

Studies by Cynthia Heald

Heald, Cynthia. *Becoming a Woman of Excellence.* Colorado Springs, CO: NavPress, 1994.

——. *Becoming a Woman of Faith.* Nashville, TN: Thomas Nelson Publishers, 2000.

——. *Becoming a Woman of Grace.* Nashville, TN: Thomas Nelson Publishers, 1998.

——. *Becoming a Woman of Prayer.* Colorado Springs, CO: NavPress, 1996.

——. *Becoming a Woman of Purpose.* Colorado Springs, CO: NavPress, 1994.

——. *Intimacy with God: A Bible Study in the Psalms.* Colorado Springs, CO: NavPress, 2000.

——. *Loving Your Husband: Building an Intimate Marriage in a Fallen World.* Colorado Springs, CO: NavPress, 2000.

Studies by Debbie Alsdorf

Alsdorf, Debbie. *Living Love: The Choice That Can Change Your Heart.* Elgin, IL: Chariot Victor Publishing, 2000.

——. *Restoring Love: Set Free to Live with Passion and Purpose.* Elgin, IL: Chariot Victor Publishing, 2001.

——. *Steadfast Love: Finding Self-Worth Through God's Truth.* Elgin, IL: Chariot Victor Publishing, 2000.

Studies by Donna Partow

Partow, Donna. *Becoming the Woman I Want to Be.* Minneapolis, MN: Bethany House Publishers, 2004.

——. *Becoming a Vessel God Can Use.* Minneapolis, MN: Bethany House Publishers, 2004.

——. *Living in Absolute Freedom.* Minneapolis, MN: Bethany House Publishers, 2000.

——. *Standing Firm.* Minneapolis, MN: Bethany House Publishers, 2001.

——. *Walking in Total God-Confidence.* Minneapolis, MN: Bethany House Publishers, 1999.

Partow, Donna, and Lin Johnson. *Extracting the Precious from II Corinthians.* Minneapolis, MN: Bethany House Publishers, 2003.

——. *Extracting the Precious from Galatians.* Minneapolis, MN: Bethany House Publishers, 2004.

——. *Extracting the Precious from Isaiah.* Minneapolis, MN: Bethany House Publishers, 2003.

——. *Extracting the Precious from Nehemiah.* Minneapolis, MN: Bethany House Publishers, 2004.

Studies by Elizabeth George

George, Elizabeth. *Becoming a Woman of Beauty and Strength: Esther.* Eugene, OR: Harvest House Publishers, 2001.

——. *Experiencing God's Peace: Philippians.* Eugene, OR: Harvest House Publishers, 2000.

——. *Growing in Wisdom and Faith: James.* Eugene, OR: Harvest House Publishers, 2001.

——. *Putting on a Gentle and Quiet Spirit: 1 Peter.* Eugene, OR: Harvest House Publishers, 2000.

Studies by Jill Briscoe

Briscoe, Jill. *Grace to Go On.* Elgin, IL: Chariot Victor Publishing, 2001.

——. *Psalms for a Woman's Life.* Elgin, IL: Chariot Victor Publishing, 1999.

——. *Understanding the Heartbeat of Jesus.* Elgin, IL: Chariot Victor Publishing, 2001.

——. *Women in the Life of Jesus.* Elgin, IL: Chariot Victor Publishing, 1999.

Studies by Kay Arthur

Arthur, Kay. *Lord, Give Me a Heart for You: A Devotional Study on Having a Passion for God.* New York: WaterBrook Press, 2001.

——. *Lord, Heal My Hurts: A Devotional Study on God's Care and Deliverance.* New York: WaterBrook Press, 2000.

——. *Lord, I Need Grace to Make It Today: A Devotional Study on God's Power for Daily Living.* New York: WaterBrook Press, 2000.

——. *Lord, I Want to Know You: A Devotional Study on the Names of God.* New York: WaterBrook Press, 2000.

——. *Lord, I'm Torn Between Two Masters: A Devotional Study on Genuine Faith from the Sermon on the Mount.* New York: WaterBrook Press, 2000.

——. *Lord, Is it Warfare? Teach Me to Stand: A Devotional Study on Spiritual Victory.* New York: WaterBrook Press, 2000.

——. *Lord, Only You Can Change Me: A Devotional Study on Growing in Character from the Beatitudes.* New York: WaterBrook Press, 2000.

——. *Lord, Teach Me to Pray in Twenty-Eight Days.* Eugene, OR: Harvest House Publishers, 2001.

——. *Lord, Where Are You When Bad Things Happen? A Devotional Study on Living by Faith.* New York: WaterBrook Press, 2000.

Video-Based Bible Studies

Moore, Beth. *A Heart Like His, Leader Kit.* Nashville, TN: LifeWay, 1996.

——. *A Woman's Heart: God's Dwelling Place, Leader Kit.* Nashville, TN: LifeWay, 1995.

——. *Beloved Disciple, Leader Kit.* Nashville, TN: LifeWay, 2002.

——. *Breaking Free: Making Liberty in Christ a Reality in Life, Leader Kit.* Nashville, TN: LifeWay, 1999.

——. *Jesus the One and Only, Leader Kit.* Nashville, TN: LifeWay, 2000.

——. *To Live Is Christ, Leader Kit.* Nashville, TN: LifeWay, 1997.

Women's Ministry E-Books

Christian, Pamela, with Rebekah Montgomery. *The Money Mission: How to Find Money for Your Women's Ministry.* Jubilant Press, 2004. http://www.finding-money.com (accessed April 14, 2004).

Porter, Karen. *Secrets to Planning a Big Event.* Jubilant Press, 2004. http://www.plan-big-event.com (accessed April 14, 2004).

Voshage, Betty. *Starting a Women's Ministry from the Ground Up.* Jubilant Press, 2004. http://www.jubilantpress.com/ebooks/ebook_women ministrygroundup.htm (accessed April 14, 2004).

New from Focus on the Family®
The Women's Ministry That Has It All!

Kit includes

- *The Focus on the Family Women's Ministry Guide*
- *Crafts and Activities for Women's Ministry*
- *Women of Worth* Bible Study
- *Healing the Heart* Bible Study
- *Balanced Living* Bible Study
- *The Blessings of Friendships* Bible Study

Focus on the Family Women's Series Kit
Group Starter Kit • Bible Study
ISBN 08307.33574
Available September 2004

Research shows that women are the backbone of Christian congregations in America,* but many are overwhelmed and in need of a break to reconnect with the Lord. Focus on the Family has **combined the best features of women's ministries**—Bible studies, prayer, fellowship, Scripture memory and activities—and created **new resources for women of all ages** so that they can *relax* and *reflect* on God.

By learning to define themselves based on God's Word, women will decrease their feelings of being inadequate and overwhelmed, and increase their sense of self-worth while joining in fellowship with God and other Christian women. Help women come together with **the new ministry that has it all!**

The Focus on the Family Women's Series
is available where Christian books are sold.

*From Barna Research, *Women Are the Backbone of the Christian Congregations in America*, March 6, 2000.

Gospel Light

We've Combined the Best of Women's Ministry for One Comprehensive Experience!

These resources provide a multitude of ideas for giving women the much-desired opportunity to get together and share different life experiences— joys and sorrows—to build deep, Christ-centered relationships.

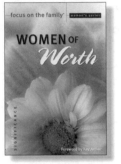

Women of Worth Bible Study

Women often define themselves by what others expect of them. Many feel they come up short when they try to have it all—beauty, family, career, success. This study helps women find their true identity and purpose through their relationship with Christ. Includes topics such as defining worth, body image, femininity, sexuality and relationships.
ISBN 08307.33361

Healing the Heart Bible Study

This study helps women experience emotional and spiritual healing by understanding the hurts and pain in their lives and finding restoration through Christ. Topics include recognizing the effects of sin, mending your thoughts, forgiveness and letting go of the past.
ISBN 08307.33620

Balanced Living Bible Study

When women strive to do it all, they end up feeling stressed out, fatigued and disconnected from God. This study gives women the tools to balance the various demands on their time while maintaining an intimate relationship with God. Topics include why women overextend themselves, separating the important from the urgent and managing the pressures of life.
ISBN 08307.33639

The Blessings of Friendships Bible Study

In today's fast-paced, busy world it's difficult for women to establish and maintain strong, healthy relationships. In this study, women will explore the nature of relationships and Christ's model for them. Some of the topics covered include forgiveness, being honest and vulnerable, the fine art of listening, receiving correction and the blessings of community.
ISBN 08307.33647

The Focus on the Family Women's Ministry Guide

This comprehensive guide gives leaders everything they need to set up and run an effective ministry for women of all ages and life situations.
ISBN 08307.33388

Crafts and Activities for Women's Ministry

This book is packed with ideas for adding fun and creativity to women's ministry meetings and special events. Includes reproducible craft patterns, activities and more!
ISBN 08307.33671

STRENGTHEN MARRIAGES.
STRENGTHEN YOUR CHURCH.

Here's Everything You Need for a Dynamic Marriage Ministry!

Group Starter Kit includes

- Nine Bible Studies: *The Masterpiece Marriage, The Passionate Marriage, The Fighting Marriage, The Model Marriage, The Surprising Marriage, The Giving Marriage, The Covenant Marriage, The Abundant Marriage* and *The Blended Marriage*
- *The Focus on the Family Marriage Ministry Guide*
- *An Introduction to the Focus on the Family Marriage Series* video

Focus on the Family ®
Marriage Series
Group Starter Kit
Kit Box
Bible Study/Marriage
ISBN 08307.32365

The overall health of your church is directly linked to the health of its marriages. And in light of today's volatile pressures and changing lifestyles, your commitment to nurture and strengthen marriages needs tangible, practical help. Now **Focus on the Family—the acknowledged leader in Christian marriage and family resources**—gives churches a comprehensive group study series dedicated to enriching marriages. Strengthen marriages and strengthen your church with **The Focus on the Family Marriage Series**.

The Focus on the Family Women's Series
is available where Christian books are sold.

Gospel Light

Welcome to the Family!

As you participate in the *Focus on the Family Women's Series*, it is our prayerful hope that God will deepen your understanding of His plan for you and that He will strengthen the women relationships in your congregation and community.

This series is just one of the many helpful, insightful, and encouraging resources produced by Focus on the Family. In fact, that's what Focus on the Family is all about—providing inspiration, information, and biblically based advice to people in all stages of life.

It began in 1977 with the vision of one man, Dr. James Dobson, a licensed psychologist and author of 18 best-selling books on marriage, parenting, and family. Alarmed by the societal, political, and economic pressures that were threatening the existence of the American family, Dr. Dobson founded Focus on the Family with one employee and a once-a-week radio broadcast aired on only 36 stations.

Now an international organization, the ministry is dedicated to preserving Judeo-Christian values and strengthening and encouraging families through the life-changing message of Jesus Christ. Focus ministries reach families worldwide through 10 separate radio broadcasts, two television news features, 13 publications, 18 Web sites, and a steady series of books and award-winning films and videos for people of all ages and interests.

We'd love to hear from you!